THE

TESTIMONY

OF

JESUS

Releasing the spirit of prophecy through Amazing Christian Testimonies & Stories

DR TIMOTHY SNG

The Testimony of Jesus – Releasing the spirit of prophecy through Amazing Christian Testimonies & Stories

Publisher: "Dr Timothy Sng"
c/o Sng Kim Hock
Taman Tun Dr Ismail, 60000 Kuala Lumpur, Malaysia
Email: timsng@gmail.com

ISBN e978-967-16824-3-2
Website/Blog: www.timsng.blogspot.com
Email: timsng@gmail.com

Cover credit: Janice Khaw   janiceaimeekhaw@gmail.com

Illustrations by: Kev Low yeefunstudio1007@gmail.com

Printers: Akitiara Sdn Bhd

This Author's Published Titles

The Good Son

E-books [Amazon]

The Good Son

How I became a Christian

The Gospel in 30 Minutes

The Instant Gospel

The Power of One Verse [Series]

The Good & Precious Wife

Once Saved Forever Safe

Anyone Can Pray

Why I am a Christian

J2C Alert

God is No Delusion

The Testimony of Jesus

Releasing the spirit of prophecy through

Amazing Christian Testimonies & Stories

Revelation 19:10

"I am your fellow servant, and of your brethren who have

the testimony of Jesus.

Worship God!

For the testimony of Jesus

is the spirit of prophecy."

This is the Testimony of Jesus
that
He is the Son of God
that
He came down on earth
born of a Virgin Birth
showed signs, wonders & miraculous healing
and declared

The Good News of Salvation for Mankind
then laid down His Life on Calvary

paying the full ransom for mankind
cleansing the sins of mankind by His Blood
so that
Whoever calls upon the Name of Jesus
will be saved.

Contents

Holy Spirit spoke: "Read Proverbs 6"

Testimony # 040
"The Photograph"

Testimony # 041
"You Shouldn't Pray Like That"

Testimony # 042
When I Asked ABBA Father

Testimony # 043
Near Collision Averted

Testimony # 044
Burst Tire Averted

Testimony # 045
Safe Landing on 8th Attempt

Testimony # 046
Possessed Live-in Maid

Testimony # 047
Ghost Family in the House

Testimony # 048
Headaches from Spirit Attacks

Testimony # 049
Oppressed Spiritually for Three Months

Testimony # 050
Gold Dusts on my Pants

Testimony # 051
I saw Manna Fall

Testimony # 052
A Hand fed me Bread

Testimony # 053
Babies are from the LORD

Testimony # 054
Mates are from the LORD

Testimony # 055
Finding Konrad

Testimony # 056
How I Found God

Testimony # 057
500 Souls Saved

Testimony # 058
Tongues & Baptism of Holy Spirit

Testimony # 059
From Coma to Life

Testimony # 060
Jesus appears to my Cousin

Testimony # 061
Instant Healing & Visitation During Prayer

Grandpa Finally Saved

Testimony # 096
Jesus my Healer

Testimony # 097
Jesus my Deliverer & Bailor

Testimony # 098
Jesus my Protector

Testimony # 099
Jesus my Savior

Testimony # 100
Jesus my Beloved

Thanksgiving

I thank Almighty God - Father & Son Jesus, for being the center of all these testimonies and stories, and the Holy Spirit of God in me, my Teacher and Counsellor.

The LORD GOD has made this book possible, and He will send it out to all the four corners of the earth.
In Him & for Him, I am made known

Thank you, *Abba Father.*

Acknowledgment

I wish to acknowledge my wonderful family – wife Jane, children Grace & David, John & Vicky and Chris & Grace, in their order of birth, now including baby Elijah Rees and Jordan Arthur for journeying with me as one household before the LORD.

This 'Good & Precious' wife of mine Jane is truly appreciated for holding the fort in almost every aspect, while I am fixed and focused on my lap top for many hours, whether day or night, often too in the early morning hours.

My daughter Grace for inspiring & contributing literally to the title, a total name and cover change. Thanks also to Janice for the awesome cover, and many more to come and to Kev for the illustrations.

Thanks to my unnamed proofreaders, who both excelled beyond 'Spelling & Grammar Check.'

Appreciation to all dear brethren who have written forwards for this book, and specially to Elder SK Ng, for allowing me to use his awesome testimony.

Grateful thanks always are due to all my pastors, our shepherds, some who have written forwards here. They have been faithful shepherds for God, covering us through trials and tribulations, a life time sacrifice indeed for the flock of God; deep gratitude and appreciation also goes to the countless teachers, who through conferences, sermons, messages, either in person or via multimedia have contributed to my own spiritual growth over the years, for faithfully feeding the flock; special personal loving thankfulness and sincere appreciation goes to the many friends and mentors, whose fellowship, advice and interaction which amount to "the great and wonderful fellowship of the saints", helpful if not necessary to make us strong, energizing one another, providing effective support to us through the times, and strengthening each other's faith as we live for Christ.

Synopsis: The Testimony of Jesus

"The Testimony of Jesus" is about testimonies encountered in my life as a Christian.

Revelation 19:10 declares that "The Testimony of Jesus is the spirit of prophecy." Thus, when testimonies are shared from one believer's heart, it releases the spirit of prophecy to activate and inspire the hearer with the prophetic word that Jesus can work miracles for you too, today.

Dr Timothy Sng shares his life experiences in personal testimonies, spread over nearly four decades, from amazing cases of healing and awakening from coma, to miraculous personal escape from near death and potentially fatal accidents, to vivid dreams where the LORD was present, glorifying God in over 100 fascinating stories.

He believes fervently that these amazing miracles are the privilege and right of every child of God, as Jesus said in John 14:12, that "you will do greater things" than He did.

The timeliness, specificity and coincidental occurrence of many of these incidents all point a Living God, as "all things are possible with God."

Be edified and inspired as you read, and you will begin to work miracles in your life, because ultimately, Jesus is the key, and center of it all.

Foreword

From my Senior Pastor

I have known Dr Timothy Sng for well over sixteen years now as his Senior Pastor, as a fellow medical colleague, but more importantly as a friend. Over the years I have seen him grow strong, resolute in his faith and in his love for Jesus. He has served faithfully in his cell, in missions to poorer countries and in speaking at many churches to encourage them. It is in this area of encouragement that Dr Sng exercises his greatest gift. He is an encourager par excellence. He always has a positive word of encouragement for widows, single parents, the hurting, the grieving and the marginalized. I have the greatest respect and admiration for Timothy, who has been a great encouragement to me personally as well. I wish for him and his loved ones all the best that Almighty God can give. I pray and believe "The Testimony of Jesus" will reach out to the ends of the earth.

Pastor Dr Chew Weng Chee
Senior Pastor & Founder, SIBKL (Sidang Injil Borneo, Kuala Lumpur)
(Formerly Obstetrician & Gynecologist)

I was reading Revelation19:10 recently, having been prompted, and for two or three days was checking the meaning of 'testimony' in the OT and 'prophecy' in the NT. During this time, a message from Brother Timothy came in, but I had delayed in reading it, until I had completed the above short study.

Imagine my surprise when I saw his book cover: **'The Testimony of Jesus'**! I can now testify to the relevance of this scripture and of this book Brother Timothy is writing.

Through the stories, there is a Golden Thread, of Him, the Anointed One, the Christ. This is the Way of the Spirit of Prophecy, Who with emergent clarity and effectiveness will build up His followers to build up followers through fresh trust, dependency and fuller knowledge of the Son in ways not seen before. Our Brother Timothy is a man of the Lord who 'walks the path in the field' where needy and hurting people are. There is definitely more to come through this writer!

Ting See Lok
Partner, TheEtsahGroup® & Managing Partner, LEAP Associates Consultancy
(Formerly Petroleum Production & Development Manager of Sabah & Sarawak Shell;
Formerly Head of Leadership Technology, Group Leadership & Performance Group,
Royal Dutch Shell)

I know this man, Dr Timothy Sng – a man who does not let the left hand know what the right hand does. Timothy is like a man whom we read in the Bible, like David, who was a man after the heart of God. He is a man who always seeks out the lost souls, and those who have backslided, with a passion to bring the Good News of Jesus Christ to the ends of the world.

My wife, Pastor Lily will testify that Dr Timothy Sng is a man of his words, and when he gives a word that he will not rest till he completes it.

Pastors Joseph & Lily Selva & Gloria Selva
Itinerant Ministers and Evangelists, Klang, Malaysia
(Pastor Joseph opened the door to ministry for the author, with his introduction and invitation to the first Full Gospel Businessman's Fellowship in the 1990s)

I have known Brother Timothy for 16 years through FGBMFI. His passion to evangelize is contagious! He will seize the opportunity to share the good news of salvation to his patients and others he meets. We have had many precious moments of fellowship, discussions and worship in the same church we belong to, SIBKL. Most precious is our work together in personal evangelism where many were saved. Please pick up a copy of this book and experience the exciting journey of evangelism and other stories of his life in the LORD.

Tan Tek Seng
Chairman, Family First Malaysia & Tyrannus Online Seminary

It is an honor to write this forward to a collection of testimonies, not just compiled by Dr Timothy, but also seen in his own life. He is one of a growing number of physicians and marketplace ministers, who are giving testimony that there is only one healer called Jesus Christ, who is our Great Physician. Dr Timothy's passion for the Lord is revealed in his passion to see souls saved and healed by the power of God, even as my late father, Dr Joy Seevaratnam, pioneered the way in the late 1970's and 1980's for other medical doctors and bi-vocational marketplace ministers in Malaysia, to be used as God's vessels of healing and deliverance to all who dare to believe in the power of the name of Jesus Christ.

The early first century New Testament church was birthed on the Day of Pentecost, when 120 supernaturally declared the wonderful works of God in languages unknown to them but known to the thousands in Jerusalem. May the wonderful works of God in this book be a light in the darkness, to help you stay in faith and hope, knowing that God is no respecter of persons, and that what He and His disciples did over 2,000 years ago, He is still doing today, freely giving you, that you may in turn freely give others what He has done for you.

May these testimonies help encourage you and build your faith, not because you are good or deserving, but because He is good, and desires to move powerfully upon you and through you, to fill your sphere of influence with the knowledge of His glory and goodness.

Reuben Seevaratnam
Global Harvest Assembly Penang, Senior Pastor
Author of "Generational Alignment - The Divine Strategy for Healing Hearts and Nations"

The Testimony of Jesus is lived through Dr Timothy Sng's life, as his testimonies tell of the wonders and miracles through Jesus, in his daily walk with his Heavenly Father. Since coming to know God in a personal relationship, Timothy has consistently strived to live his life and walk in a way as a good son to bring glory to his Father.

Pastor Tony Tan,
Chairman & Adviser
Creation Community International AG, Malaysia.
(Author's former Pastor at Lifeline AOG Church, Kuala Terengganu, Malaysia,1982-1988)

Dr Timothy Sng is a man of action and sacrifice, in bringing souls to Christ. His zeal and passion never waivers nor lessen year by year. Instead they grow stronger and more committed. We all can learn a lot from his fine example and from his second book "Testimony of Jesus" to fulfil God's will in our life.

His Christ-like gentle, helpful, considerate character and wisdom is a 'magnet', drawing and touching many who are searching for the truth. We pray that God will use this humble servant of His to revolutionize and motivate many disciples to win more souls for His Glory and Honor. If everyone imitates and live our lives like Timothy to win souls, the whole earth will reverberate with His glory.

Pastor David Liew Chee Kien
Pastor (English Section) Saving Grace Church,
Kepong, Kuala Lumpur, Malaysia

I have known Dr Timothy Sng since 2005. He is a generous tent-maker, and supporter of smaller churches like GISM (Gereja Injil Sepenuh Malacca). Since I have known him, Dr Sng has always responded to requests for urgent needs or support. His deep concern for the church of Christ, and servants of the LORD, his humility and ever ready assistance has been a tremendous encouragement to me and my service to God. We deeply appreciate and value his help and contributions, with gratitude, and wish him all the best in this endeavor as an author of "The Testimony of Jesus". May God bless Dr Sng with manifold blessings for all his good work and generosity.

Pastor Vincent Tharuman Maniam
Senior Pastor, Gereja Injil Sepenuh, Sri Aman, Sarawak
(Translated: Full Gospel Church, Sarawak, formerly Senior Pastor GIS, Malacca)

Dr Timothy is a dedicated neurologist, a faithful husband to one wife, a loving father of three children and a good friend for many, both in his home land and around the globe. More than anything, he is a true 'lover of God.'

He was introduced to me not as a doctor, but as a 'friend of God' and there began our friendship more than a decade ago. I find that his zeal for God is vibrant, his love for God is unconditional, his faith in Him is ever increasing and his heart for the ministry and the ministers of God is ever expanding. He is one who keeps himself ready to speak for God in and out of season. I see him running his race of life as he continues his good fight of faith for God.

I commend his book on testimonies in his life – "The Testimony of Jesus."

Reverend Edward Francis
Senior Pastor, Bread of Life Church, Manipal, India.

I had the privilege to know Dr Timothy Sng from 1989, when he visited me in New Delhi, and again on my trips to Malaysia. I know he is a child of GOD, a man of GOD, and a bible student, as well as teacher with a passion to walk the talk first. This new title sharing a hundred personal testimonies will surely reveal "Jesus". It is birthed after decades of walking with the LORD. The experiences he has gone through with the Lord is clearly an inspiration for all , who desire to be a true disciple of the Lord and to live a victorious Christian life, and in work place. I strongly recommend this book to all who have a passion to grow in Christ.

dr p.g.vargis
founder and chief mentor, Indian Evangelical Team, India
(Author: IET has planted over 10,000 churches, mainly in North India and neighboring region.)

Dr Timothy Sng has been friends of Prince of Peace Ministry, India, and personal friends of me and my family for two decades. Apart from coordinating meetings and having fellowship during my ministry trips to Malaysia, he has visited Prince of Prince head church, several village churches and our prayer mountain, ministering to the flock wherever he went. His support, encouragement, prayers and commitment for Prince of Peace Ministries over two decades is deeply appreciated. As a co-laborer for the Kingdom of God, I thank God for his heart and passion. He is indeed an exemplary Marketplace minister and I commend Dr Tim's work as author of 'The Testimony of Jesus' to you.

Bishop BA Santhosam
Founder & Bishop, Prince of Peace, India
(Prince of Peace India has over 350 village churches in South India)

I have known Dr Sng for a good number of years now. He has a tremendous heart for God and His Kingdom. God uses him greatly to advance the gospel by sharing the Word in the market places and also supporting many ministries and ministers.

Timothy indeed is a true friend and a co-laborer in the Kingdom of God. He has great passion too for mission and missionaries. God anoints him for understanding the Word and also receiving revelation from God. A man of integrity and one who walks in the fear of God, this book affirms a lifelong walk with the LORD. I strongly recommend "The Testimony of Jesus" for the works of ministry. He truly is God ordained for such a time as we approach the coming and arrival of our Lord Jesus Christ.

Pastor George G.A.Thevarakam
Itinerant Minister, Kingdom Faith Fellowship International

Dr Tim is a man after God's very own heart. Despite his busy schedule he always finds the time to share the Gospel, at every opportunity, so that many can come to know and receive Christ as their Lord and Savior.

May this new book: 'The Testimony of Jesus' touch many hearts and souls for Jesus.

Evangelist & Tentmaker Philip Ong
Go Forth Asia Board member, FGB Sunway Chapter President, and Gideons Petaling Jaya Camp President, Malaysia

It is my joy to commend Dr Timothy Sng to you. We were classmates in school in Kluang, Johor from 1958 to 1962, and reconnected only recently. I admire Dr Sng for his integration of Christian life with his professional life. He lives out a lifestyle of witness and testimony in church and ministry. He is also well known professionally with patients coming from many countries. Matthew 5:16 best reflects his life: as doctor, writer, evangelist, friend, and preacher.

I commend this book on his life's testimonies: "The Testimony of Jesus."

Reverend Dr M G George
Pastor of Malaysia Discipleship Center churches (1968-2016).
Currently, Pastor, Johor Bahru Disciples Church, Malaysia

We have known Dr Timothy Sng personally for more than ten years. Not only is he an outstanding neurologist, but he really is a man after God's heart. Always ready to testify to God's love through his own experiences, Dr Sng is a fine example of one who not only preaches the Word but one who lives the Word.

We warmly recommend him and his writings in "The Testimony of Jesus", which will be a blessing to those who will have open hearts.

Reverend Steve Chang & Lily Chang
Senior Pastor, River of Life Sanctuary
Desa Sri Hartamas, Kuala Lumpur

In my opinion, Dr S'ng is a person who has a great burden for lost souls, with a deep agape love for those dear to him. For many years, I have witnessed the price he has paid for the salvation of some of these precious loved ones. Often, in order for Jesus to be glorified, he persevered and endured, looking up to the love of the Heavenly Father and the mercy of Jesus Christ. By the power granted to him by the Holy Spirit, Dr S'ng has been able to hold on to the present, and still not give up.

He is steadfast in his conviction of God's promises, and he tries his best to satisfy the Father's expectations of him. He believes that the difficulties and trials he has experienced has given him patience and a strong mind, and thus continues to run along the narrow path for the glory of the Father and the exaltation of the Lord Jesus Christ!

I begin to see that the prophetic word released years ago on this servant's writing and works in Christian literature is being fulfilled with "The Testimony of Jesus".

Reverend (Ms) Crystal Cheang
Crystalsea Prophetic Ministry, Author of "Wonderful Trip to Heaven"
Itinerant Minister, Dream Center, Ipoh, Malaysia

It has been a pleasure knowing Dr Timothy Sng over 14 years now. He is a wonderful doctor, and a great friend to all our family members. He models how we can face challenges with confidence and faith and he willingly communicate valuable lessons from his life experiences. This book is for all who desire to live out a well transformed life, drawing close to the Father, and seeing miracles in their daily walk.

Pastor (Ms) Inky Ong
Senior Pastor SIBKLCC, (Chinese Church) Kuala Lumpur

Brother Sng Kim Hock (Timothy) is passionate in reaching out to many in the market place fulfilling the Great Commission. He is a great encourager who ministers in the power of the Holy Spirit. A humble servant of God, a prayerful son, full of grace and compassion like his Master.

Elder Dr. Ng Soon Gan
Elder & Past Chairman, Full Gospel Assembly, Kuala Lumpur

I have known Dr Sng for more than 20 years. He has a tremendous heart for God and His Kingdom. God uses him greatly to advance the gospel by preaching the Word in the market places and also supporting (with his co-laborers) financially many ministries. Dr Sng has great passion too for both mission and missionaries. God anoints him for understanding the Word and also receiving revelation from God.
He seeks fervently after prophetic gifting and teaching, attending many seminars by apostles, prophets and teachers from all over the world, that come from USA, UK, India to bless many people in the region. As a man of integrity, he walks in the fear of God. I highly recommend him for ministry.

Dr Paul Ang
Founder Paul Ang Global Vision Ministry, former Pastor, Tabernacle of Glory, Kuala Lumpur, Malaysia

Dr Timothy is a very close friend of my father, the Late Reverend Dr P.N.Samy Davis, Founder of Jesus Loves Ministries, with 18 branch churches in Malaysia. Dr Timothy himself has led over 500 souls to Christ, through direct personal evangelism, especially in the marketplace. Dr Timothy preaches the Word of God in a very inspiring and encouraging way. The move of the Holy Spirit is evident in his ministry. A man full of God's love, he shows patience, demonstrates love through his deeds, supporting the ministry of God in many ways. May God bless his work exceedingly.

Reverend (Ms) Malina Davis Alfred
Co-President, Jesus Loves Ministries, Malaysia

As Dr Tim Sng's former Pastor in SIB Iris Garden, Kuching, Sarawak, it gives me great joy to know how the Lord has used him in the last 30 over years. I have known Tim to be a compassionate man with a passion for the lost. The angels in heaven rejoice in each person he led to know Jesus through this, His humble servant.

The Lord has given Tim the gift of an evangelist, confirmed in his effective ministry of bringing so many to the saving knowledge of Jesus. I look forward to "The Testimony of Jesus", and to be inspired by another servant of the Lord.

Reverend Osh Ong
Former Senior Pastor, Chinese Church, London & Ambassador of Tearfund,
Evangelical Alliance, Global Connections & COCM, United Kingdom
(Author's former Pastor, SIB Iris Garden, Kuching, Sarawak, Malaysia)

Dr Timothy Sng, truly an evangelist is a person who has a great burden for lost souls. He is following the Great Commission by actively reaching out to as many people as he can, so as to bring them in to full knowledge of Salvation (1 Timothy 2:4). He has such a burning desire for all humanity to be delivered and come to full knowledge of The Truth. He also actively supports ministers and those people in desperate need both locally and internationally. I attest that Dr Timothy is a humble and a compassionate man who truly loves our Lord and Master, The King of kings - Yeshua Hamashiach.

Bishop Dr Yeheqel Panier Selvam
Overseer, Supernatural Breakthrough Assembly, Kuala Lumpur
Emissary United Christian Assembly

"Call upon Me and I will answer you " Jeremiah 33:3

Father God heard me and sent His messenger Dr Timothy Sng Kim Hock, Consultant Neurologist.

I first met Timothy very soon after I had lost my wife (Bishop) Diana in 2007. We met at a Christian conference, and immediately engaged in fellowship. Somehow, the Lord led me to share my sorrow with this younger brother, who instantaneously comforted me with his arms warmly around my shoulder, praying touching words that ministered to my grieving soul.

On another occasion, when I was in my distress, Timothy Sng flew into Singapore from Kuala Lumpur, and spent time on my side, praying and restoring my brokenness, with the Word to confess. Luke 1:37 "For with God, nothing will be impossible".

Thirty years on, this Word has been my compass and standard bearer perpetually and perennially, as the 'Good Samaritan' Timothy had declared to me.

Years later, and now, obedient at 90 years of age, I stand on as the Monk Martin Luther on the promises of God. Since that very first encounter with this man of God, we have kept in touch, and our friendship blossomed. It would be no coincidence that Timothy would befriend my daughter Oweeniya and husband Devan, and later be at Devan's bedside to minister prayers of healing. Again, Timothy would visit, pray and encourage me when I was unwell in Kuala Lumpur.

After the tragic loss of my family home to fire, we saw countless miracles coming our way. My late wife, Diana saw the birth of the ICAG, - International Christian Ambassadors of God (a council of churches and fellowships), which grew and spread over four continents. In obedience to the Great Commission out lined in the full Gospels, we travelled far and wide spreading the Good News and winning souls. Just as in Isaiah 61.3, the Spirit of the Lord had anointed us to preach the Good News to the poor, lost and needy.

Again, we connected in October 2019, when Timothy came and ministered to the ICAG 10th Annual Conference in Batam.

Indeed, at 90 years of age, standing as a veteran of 50 years in missions I was moved through reading Dr Timothy Sng's first book, "The Good Son", and his gift in authorship continues in "The Testimony of Jesus."

Indeed, let us all together "Make a joyful noise unto the Lord" (Psalm 100).

"In Him, I live and, in Him I move, and in Him, I have my being." Acts 17:28

Yours in His service,

Dr. Eugene Melchizedek Owen
Patriarch and former Archbishop ICAG, Council of Churches
Dip. Tung Ling Bible College, Singapore
Ph.D. Missiology Bristol U.K., M.Ed. USA.

"**Can a follower** of Jesus Christ run a business in the marketplace and yet at the same time live out his fervent passion for lost souls?"

It is an unequivocal "YES!" This is a remarkable and amazing story of Dr Timothy Sng, a person with an unwavering zeal for the Lord Jesus Christ and overflowing with passion for lost souls. What makes him unique is that he operates a medical practice in the marketplace and yet has shown an incredible tenacity to exercise faith in aligning and integrating his medical practice with 'doing the Father's Business' of touching and transforming people's lives while earning a living in the marketplace. He is a walking and living testimony that the invisible walls between the secular and the sacred need not be there. The competency of his medical skills blend with his heart and passion for lost souls have remodeled his everyday life to live it holistically to touch the lives of ordinary people that Dr Timothy encounters daily in the marketplace. This book will challenge us to bring the power of God's presence to our workplace and experience miracles in our business.

Yaw Chun Soon
Executive Director, Talam Transform Berhad and
Head of Workplace Ministry, SIBKL, Malaysia

Timothy Sng Endorsement

Timothy Sng has been a great friend over many years. He is one of the rare breed who accomplishes much in God's Kingdom "under the radar screen". His zeal for the Lord has never diminished, his love for people and his compassion for the needy are remarkable. Attached to that is an unflinching faith that God is able to do outstanding miracles today and you have a life that sizzles with the extraordinary! In that sense our journey as medical specialists are very similar. This book will fire your spirit and recharge you to desire more of Jesus.

Pastor Dr. Philip Lyn
Consultant Physician
Senior Pastor, Skyline SIB
Kota Kinabalu

[Footnote: I am touched and even `flattered' by the many words of recognition and acknowledgement even praise directed towards me, though it is my LORD who is truly deserving of all praise, honor and glory. I continue to take up Reverend Watchman Nee's Motto for my life:

"I want everything for my LORD; I want nothing for myself"

If I am exalted, it is He who exalts me, and I continue to breathe and exist for His Glory, to further glorify His Name and extend His Glorious Kingdom, on earth as well as in Heaven.]

Preface

"The Testimony of Jesus" as a title was birthed overnight, and delivered within three months, though the content covers testimonies from nearly four decades of my life in Christ. God-given ideas in the form of 'titles' to write often pop up in my mind during this recent season. "The Good Son" (to be republished under a new title "Pleasing our Father in Heaven" was one such title, birthed overnight and delivered within six months.

Almost all testimonies are personally experienced by this author, while a few were told directly to me by the witnesses themselves. The last eight from #93 to # 100 are my personal testimonies to my Lord Jesus, Who is "the Way, the Truth and the Life."

 "The Testimony of Jesus" will stir you, inspire and provoke you, a believer in Jesus Christ to see miracles and powerful working of the Spirit of God in your life. This is the intended and true purpose of testimonies, that in glorifying God, the Spirit of God will move in ministry and do the Mighty works of God in your life too, even as you are reading these stories.

I was sharing on the 19th of July 2019, at one Full Gospel Businessman Fellowship lunch meeting pouring out testimony after testimony, from my heart declaring the goodness of the LORD, when one brother Sebastian Cheng heard, and received one particular testimony with great joy.

Exactly a month later, I met him at the Asian Beacon Anniversary dinner on 18th August 2019, where I was a guest of my cousin Joanne, Sebastian told me that he had gone on to retell the same testimony #47, over and over again, and at last count over a dozen times and many listeners were blessed.

It was that brief word of encouragement from Brother Sebastian that triggered my inner man to take up this project, guided by the Holy Spirit. Thus, project was birthed on the night of the 18th August 2019! I have no doubt that it is Holy Spirit, my Teacher, Counsellor and Miracle Co-worker, who inspired me along, for within three months, the "Testimony of Jesus" was ready for press.

I love to tell testimonies, and testimonies are undeniably powerful in giving glory to God, for they are real and they speak of the goodness of God, our Father in Heaven. In all humility, it is not for my fame, name or personal gain, but for the Glory of God, testifying to the goodness of God, as we have all received through His Son and Savior Jesus Christ.

Unless stated as true actual names, the identities of most of the names are not revealed, using fictitious ones, and hence any similarities in the names mentioned may be coincidental. I would like to thank Elder SK Ng (# 029 'Another Tsunami Story – Nearly washed away') for allowing me to use and publish his family's testimony, and also to many others who have allowed their names to be mentioned.

Just before publication, my daughter Grace came up with the title: "The Testimony of Jesus", quoting from Revelation 19:10, and added "Releasing the spirit of prophecy through **Amazing Christian Testimonies & Stories**" – the latter in bold, being the original title.

Soon after this title was chosen, about a month before the publication, I found Bill Johnson's 2014 book "Releasing the Spirit of Prophecy" hitting a similar note. I purchased the Kindle version, and have begun reading it just a month before my draft was to be submitted to the press.

The first few paragraphs of the first chapter 'Truth Empowers' opened my understanding to Revelation 19:10, and guided by the Holy Spirit, wrote the second Chapter expounding this same verse. I acknowledge and attribute Reverend Bill Johnson for opening my own spiritual eyes through the first few pages of his book above. Hence, I have deliberately stopped reading at the very first chapter until my book is released, and will pick up to read it once "The Testimony of Jesus" is published.

Thus, due credit goes to Grace, my daughter for proposing the title of this book, and to Reverend Bill Johnson for the awesome insight of Revelation 19:10, which I received from the just the first few paragraphs of his book.

I believe that when the reader reads these testimonies, the spirit of prophecy will speak to them that they too can do the works of God, as the Holy Spirit acts as a catalyst to inspire hundreds and thousands of testimonies all for the Glory of God. I welcome your testimonies as a feedback.

Testimonies are "declarations of truth and fact" no different from sworn evidence given by a witness, delivered under oath. In court, they have the power to convict and sentence one to death, or set another free. Equally if not more then, these testimonies of Jesus have the power to deliver the reader and hearer, through the working of the spirit of prophecy, so that people will be set free as they hear these testimonies of Jesus, to believe and accept Jesus as Savior and be healed, delivered and set free.

Truly, this is "The Testimony of Jesus" lived out in this humble servant's life of nearly four decades in the LORD. May it release the spirit of prophecy as you read 'amazing Christian testimonies and stories', so that you will see and experience miracles today. And, keep testifying to the goodness and the greatness of our LORD, as the Hebrew root word "edah" says, "keep doing it", forever and forever, all for His Glory.

Jesus said in John 14:12 "Greater works than these he (you) will do, because I go to My Father."

Humbly, on His Majesty's Service

Dr Timothy Sng

The Power of Testimonies

Testimonies of the saints – believers, followers and disciples of Jesus Christ are awesome and powerful.

Searching for the word 'testimony' in the New King James Version, I found 90 verses, from Old to New Testament, with equal number of verses in each Old and New Testament.

As for the plural 'testimonies', there were 37 verses, all of which were in the Old Testament except for one in the New Testament.

The first references in Exodus 16:34 and Exodus 25:16, and again in verses 21&22 refer to the covenant by God to us, noted later in the "Two Tablets of Testimony", kept in the ark of the Testimony or the Tabernacle. In the Old Testament, almost all the verses refer to God's covenant with man.

In the New Testament, Jesus referred to the man who was healed that by showing himself to the priest and offering a gift to the priest, it was a testimony or witness to them, that he was healed. [Matthew 8:4]

Again, in Matthew 10:18, Jesus referred to the believers and followers that the process of persecution will involve them being brought before the governors and kings, and hence a 'testimony' from the follower will be presented to the authorities.

John 3:33 asserts that "He who has received His testimony has certified that God is true."

1 John 5:11 says, "And this is the testimony that God has given up eternal life, and this life is in His Son."

Testimonies are powerful, as quoted in **Revelation 12:11, "And they overcame him by the blood of the Lamb and by the word of their testimony, and they did not love their lives to the death."**

Testimonies are stories of events with descriptions as it has happened. There should not be any room for doubt, or query, and its authenticity is based on the story teller's integrity and honesty. Unbelief or doubt, when it lingers in one, will quench the Holy Spirit and hence reduce the power of God working in one's life, whether in prayer, or in seeing miracles and healing. Hence, one of this author's frequent prayer is, "LORD, help my unbelief!"

When one expresses gratitude to God, declaring His goodness over our lives, seeking forgiveness, praying, "LORD, help my unbelief!" or declaring "I believe, LORD; I believe", the door is open for the working of miracles. Our faith makes the difference as after all, our prayer ends with an 'Amen', which means "I believe".

The Hebrew word for testimony is 'edah', from the root word 'ad, coming from the letters *ayin* and *dalet.* In the settings of ancient times, it means to "see or observe the door". As the door of the house is the most repeatedly used part of the whole structure, even the key channel, where we are constantly "going in and out", we can interpret and extrapolate or expand the "act of testifying" or giving testimony as "to do it again repeatedly", or like the door, testimonies are to be repeated, daily and regularly.

Thus, to testify, according to the meaning of the root word means to observe (hear) and to repeat the same action. The Hebrew language, being cyclical also translate it as "as forever and ever ".

May this author pray with you:

"Father God, even as these testimonies are shared from my heart to the reader, hearer and listener, may you speak to each one, quicken their spirits to hear and receive, and to believe in the Lordship of Jesus, Your Son, that He is the Savior of mankind, the redeemer of our sins, the Way and the Truth and the Life; I pray that this seed of truth, and the power of these testimonies planted and sowed into their hearts will grow their faith and belief, so that each one too will work the same, and even greater miracles of healing, faith, and power, all for God's Glory. We pray this prayer in the Mighty and Awesome Name of Jesus. Amen."

The Testimony of Jesus & The Spirit of Prophecy

Revelation 19:10 says "The testimony of Jesus is the spirit of prophecy"

Every testimony below is about Jesus.

Jesus said, "without Me you can do nothing." Literally, and figuratively, we are totally dependent on our Lord & Master Jesus in everything we do. He is the energy, the source, the operating system of the earth and whatever therein.

Just as we use the Windows Operating system in Microsoft and all the applications cannot function without the Windows Operating system, likewise "planet earth functions with the operating system from which all things were made i.e. Jesus Christ.

John 1:3 declares, "All things were made through Him, and without Him nothing was made that was made."

Yet, with God, all things are possible. [Mark 10:27]

This means that all these testimonies are about Jesus, and all these miracles and wonders happened because Jesus made it possible.

Hence, and therefore, these are indeed, **"The Testimony of Jesus".**

Now, comes the powerful connection or interface between the two powerful truths i.e. that **"The testimony of Jesus is the spirit of prophecy".**

I paraphrase and extend the sentence to explain the full meaning and power in this short segment of verse Revelation 19:10, which I received as an insight for the first time, from reading Bill Johnson's book.

The testimonies that we, His saints share about the great workings and miracles of God in our lives is the catalyst, trigger and inspiration that will spark faith in the hearer and believer, for by testifying to a Living God who is still working miracles in our lives , it releases a prophetic word to be received and acted upon by the hearer.

Simply put, it means, "Jesus did this in my life; He can do it in your life too; He will do it in your situation too!"

In other words, "the testimonies about Jesus effectively releases the prophetic word in the hearers' life, and empowers them to activate and lift their faith to a higher level and see miracles of God take place."

"The testimony about Jesus is the key to release the spirit of prophecy, in the form of a prophetic word for the hearer that God has done this, and can do it for me too!"

"The testimony of Jesus enables the release of the spirit of prophecy to the hearer."

For me, each testimony I experience takes me on a higher plane that affirms to me and my spirit that my LORD is with me, all the days of my life. Jesus is my Savior; Jesus continues to save me from danger; Jesus will save me from all situations.

Here are some examples of this truth that "The Testimony of Jesus is the spirit of prophecy."

Jesus healed the ten lepers **(Testimony of Jesus)**; Jesus will heal you of your serious skin and bone disease, whatever you are suffering from since leprosy was an incurable and disfiguring disease, one of the worst sickness at that time (**Spirit of Prophecy** released through the prophetic word).

Jesus raised Lazarus from the dead **(Testimony of Jesus)**, and Jesus raised Dr Peng from the coma and near death (# 006 Messenger in the Fog, another **Testimony of Jesus**), so Jesus will raise your comatose, dying family member (**Spirit of Prophecy** released through the prophetic word).

The man of God was going for an operation that cost him almost forty-five thousand Malaysian ringgit (10,000 USD), and indeed God provided for it and more in # 019 The Cup Overflows **(Testimony of Jesus);** He will surely bail you out of your financial debts. (**Spirit of Prophecy** released through the prophetic word).

You didn't study hard enough for the examinations, and did not deserve great results but God can turn it around for you (# 080 God's Eraser–From One to Seven Distinctions).

You were in real danger, a life and death situation, but the Lord Jesus can deliver you (# 001 Saved from Beheading through the Name of Jesus & # 012 Adrift in Pacific Ocean). Jesus did it for Mr Tam, and me; He will do it for you too.

A hard-core atheist can believe just through a believer's prayer; your prayer can move your beloved friend or relative's heart to believe too (# 063 From Atheist to Believer).

A twelve-year old girl, barely twelve hours as a believer calling upon the Name of Jesus can deliver a whole family from demons; you too can move mountains (# 047 Ghost Family in the House).

The testimonies of Jesus's powerful miracles will release the spirit of prophecy that you can see the same miracles in your life too. The Testimony of Jesus effectively releases the Spirit of Prophecy, through the prophetic word given or claimed by the hearer.

"He did it before, He can do it, and will do it again for me."

My daughter Grace has this testimony:

"I was living in the United Kingdom from 1999-2006. I came across Loren Cunningham's book on 'Daring to Live on the Edge' – The Adventure on Faith and Finances, and was reading the testimony of a minister who went on a trip by faith successfully in the United States with only 50c in his pocket at the start of his journey.

When I read that testimony, my faith rose as I said, "LORD, surely this could also happen to me too." On that same day, my thoughts then focused on a good Christian conference in UK about to take place over the next few days. I was very keen to go for that conference, but it would have cost me £200 Sterling pounds, at a time when my finances were critical. I told the LORD that it was a lot of money that can be used for greater needs as in feeding the poor and orphans.

The LORD spoke to me, almost within the hour, "My child, I have more than enough to feed all the poor children and also provide for your conference." With that strong affirmation from the LORD, I decided to 'sign up' for the conference.

I was then staying with Aunty Tina, a cousin of my dad. After a short walk in the park, reflecting on the words from the LORD, when I got home that evening, Aunty passed me an envelope and said, "Grace, this is for you."

I politely declined, but Aunty insisted. I thanked her with a grateful heart, knowing in my spirit that it was going to match the conference fee.

I opened the envelope in my bedroom and I saw inside exactly £200 sterling cash.

The testimony of Jesus is indeed the spirit of prophecy!

Grace Sng."

As you read these testimonies, cry out to God and say:

"I believe! I receive! Do it for me too, Jesus! Save me! Heal me! Help me! Send your angels to minister to my loved ones. Holy Spirit of God (Spirit of Christ), convict my unbelieving family member today, even now!"

May the Testimony of Jesus activate the spirit of prophecy in your life today.

Testimony # 001

Saved from Beheading through the Name of Jesus

Mr. Tam, a Malaysian Chinese elderly man was in his mid-eighties, when he came to see me in my clinic, about fifteen years ago.

He said, "Doc, by the way, I want to tell you my story, and what happened to me during the Japanese Occupation of Malaya."

The Japanese occupied Malaya between 1941-1945, and Mr. Tam was then in his twenties.

"I was an active member of the resistance against the Japanese, called the MPAJA or Malayan Peoples' anti-Japanese Army. Unfortunately, I and my friends were caught."

For those who are not fully aware of the history of the Japanese invasions, Japan had already invaded China and the 'Massacre of Nanking' or the "Rape of Nanking" which took place over six weeks between December 1937 to January 1938 had left between 50,000 to 300,000 Chinese people dead, and between 20,000 to 80,000 women raped.

The fresh memories of the horrors of that evil tragedy had sunk deep into the hearts of the Malayan people in particular the Chinese, and news spread rapidly across South East Asia, even in the era where multimedia was non-existent. That background led to the formation of MPAJA, as arch rivals of the Japanese, and naturally the Malayan Chinese became targets of the Japanese more than the other races.

"I was scheduled for execution by beheading. One day, on a sunny midday, I was taken out to be executed. My friends' heads had already rolled into the basket. It was my turn. Kneeling down, blindfolded, I cried out with all heart, "JESUS, JESUS, help!!!""

"Immediately, all of a sudden, on that sunny day, a heavy downpour took place instantly, and all of us, both the executioner, me and others ran into the building for cover."

"I was relieved that my execution was deferred and postponed. Jesus had saved my life in the nick of time."

"The weather was wet and rainy for a few more days. On the fourth or fifth day, it was sunny again, and they decided to begin another round of execution. Again, my comrades ahead of me were beheaded."

"My turn came again. Kneeling down, blind-folded, I cried out with all my heart again, "JESUS, JESUS, help me!!!""

"Heavy thunderstorms and downpour of rains took place instantly again, exactly like the first time, a few days before. All of us ran helter-skelter for cover into the building."

"I was brought before the Japanese platoon commander. The executioners related the story about me, crying for help from Jesus, and twice instantly heavy rain had poured down suddenly on each sunny day."

"The commander looked at me with shock and spoke in Japanese, saying that 'this man is divine' [Kimoyona! Kono otoko wa kamidesu!]; we cannot kill him. Release him and let him go!"

"So, I was released!"

[What an awesome testimony! We give God all the praise and glory!!]

His son, a member of my church was with him, listening to the testimony intently.

I turned to look at his son, and remarked, "That is an amazing testimony. Has your father ever told you about it?"

"No, I am hearing it for the first time!" the son said.

I took out my hand phone, then looked at Mr Tam, and said, "Tell me your story again, and I am going to record it on video. Why have you not told others about your amazing miracle about how Jesus saved you from being beheaded?"

I have since kept a short video recording of this awesome testimony.

I then told him, "God has preserved your life. Go and tell people this testimony of how the LORD has saved you from death."

What I received personally from this testimony:

"The Name of Jesus is awesome and powerful!"
"Call unto Jesus whenever you are in trouble. God is timely in answering our prayers. He is never slow or slack."

Testimony # 002   Jesus Finds my Long-Lost Friend

It was one of my trips to Perth. I had just landed on the tarmac in Perth.

I was there for a short few days to attend a conference and we were staying at a beach side hotel called, "Scarborough Hotel", if I recall correctly.

On entering the airport terminal, I had a very strong desire to meet a couple whom I have not met for fifteen years. I had known them when I was posted to Sibu, Sarawak for a short posting in the mid-eighties.

All I could recall was that they were in Perth and he was sent there as the resident pastor of a Chinese Methodist church. Albert and Elizabeth Chiew were their names.

My silent prayer or earnestness from my heart was, "Lord Jesus, I want to meet Albert and Elizabeth. I have not seen them for 15 years. Where are they, Lord?"

How does one search for a couple in a city, when all you have is a name? I had a very deep sense of belief and trust that I would find them, or at least Albert.

I did not go out very much, as our meeting was held on site in Scarborough Hotel.

On the third day, around lunch time, as I was walking around the buffet hall, choosing from the delicacies displayed, a man tapped me on my shoulder and asked:

"Are you Dr Sng?"

I turned around and looked. To my surprise, it was Albert, right there in front of me, staring at me. I had found Albert, and it was Albert who had recognized me after fifteen years.

God had answered the desire of my heart. [Psalm 37.4] I was face to face with Albert!

I prayed and thanked God that I had found and met Albert! Or, to put it correctly, God had sent him to me!

Albert, or Reverend Albert then shared with me, that despite his fifteen years in Perth, it was the first time he had stepped his foot in this particular hotel. He went on to say that he was there because it was a farewell lunch given in his honor by some members of his church, as by the next week, he would be off to Sydney, for his next posting, which was a move after fifteen years.

Now, how does one explain this coincidence and timing that we should meet on his last week in Perth, in a hotel that he has never been to, and that the farewell party was scheduled there while I was there!?

I know it in my heart that it has to be God, who engineered it and found me my long, long friend! This testimony has really raised my faith almost literally to the point that I have that deep faith that God is my divine "finder" and also my divine "appointment scheduler."

What I have learned from this testimony:

God gives us the desires of our heart. Psalms 37:4. When, we have a deep yearning, a deep longing or desire, we can be assured the LORD will grant us the desires of our heart.

There is a Friend who is patiently seeking out for you.

Testimony # 003   Jesus Standing beside me

I have not seen a vision of my Lord Jesus, but these following short testimonies remind me that He is indeed by my side.

One well known and acknowledged prophet from South India, while praying over me said that Jesus was walking by my side during my work in the workplace.

This testimony happened when I visited a man of God, Reverend Jesudason in Malacca, a town in Malaysia. He is the same man of God in the testimony # 074 "Jesudason came to my Clinic."

As soon as I walked into his home, his grandson, a four-year-old boy remarked, "Tata (grandpa), Jesus there!"

"Where?" Grandpa asked.

"Beside Uncle", pointing at me, as the grandson said.

I was there with my son, John on a social visit. After we left, Reverend Jesudason asked his grandson a few more questions.

"How did Jesus look like?"

The boy said, "Very beautiful."

"Did Jesus have a beard?"

The boy said, "No", - presumably referring to the absence of flowing long beard from the chin.

Children of that age speak the truth and do not lie. I was touched, moved and edified that the Lord Jesus was with me, on my right-hand side.

On another occasion, I was visiting Bishop James Santhosam, Founder of Prince of Peace in South India, and was praying for his ailing wife. While Pastor himself had seen Jesus on many occasions, his wife had not.

As I leaned over to pray, she said, "I see the face of Jesus."

I am just an ordinary servant, and nowhere compared to the long-dedicated ministry of Bishop James, but the Lord Jesus chose me to represent Him at that point of contact. Both the woman of God and me were strongly encouraged. She has since gone home to be with Jesus.

A third situation was in my consultation room, while I was sharing the 'Good News' to an Indonesian Chinese man. He had responded very quickly, and said the 'sinner's prayer, surrendering his life to Jesus, very soon after a short chat. After the prayer of commitment to the Lord, and having congratulated him on his decision to receive Jesus as his Savior, I asked him: "How come you could easily believe and receive Jesus as your Savior."

He answered, "Doc, I saw Jesus standing behind you, a moment ago."

I know for sure that the Lord Jesus is by our side, all the time, even as I minister to others. This is true not just for me, but for everyone who believes.

The Word is clear in **Psalm 16:8 "I have set the LORD always before me: Because He is at my right hand I shall not be moved."**

What can we know from this testimony?

You may not see, hear, or even feel the presence of Jesus beside you. The truth is that He is by our side. Jesus, our Friend walks beside me always.

Many years ago, there was a movement called WWJD or a question for believers to ask themselves, "What would Jesus do?" in that situation. Here, the truth is He is already by your side, and therefore, surely you would not be doing what you should not do, nor go where you should not be going.

Testimony # 004   Jesus Helps me Escape

Dreams are very real to me, and as the dreamer, I know when the dreams are from God.

The Lord Jesus appeared in my dreams at least twice.

In the first dream, I was a 'marked' man, and was being hunted down by the 'Mob'. Members of the mob were dressed in black, wore shades and carried what looked like machine guns. They had a very clear and specific goal: "to hunt me down." It was quite a helpless feeling to be hunted down, as I was a fugitive or someone on the run.

I was walking in a public area, where there were crowds of people. These men in black suits were there, looking high and low for me, and asking about 'me', searching for me. I was very careful not to be discovered. Yet, I sensed the danger that I was very close to being found, and that would be fatal for me. I was defenseless, and did not carry any weapons with me. In the dream, I was in fact just an ordinary person, moving around alone.

I decided that that city was too dangerous for me, so I took off and flew into another city, where I thought I would be safe. On arrival in the next city, I was shocked to see lots of men in black suits there too, again all also looking out for me. It was like a scene from 'Matrix'.

It was quite a frightening feeling when one is being hunted down, and I knew that sooner or later, I would be caught. There did not seem to be any place on earth that was safe.

Suddenly, a 'Man' appeared to me and spoke to me, reassuringly.

He said gently, comfortingly and in a very authoritative and reassuring tone, "Come, do not worry. Let me show you how to evade them." He literally walked with me through the crowds, arm around my shoulder, with the men in black were clearly around everywhere did not see me. Without any mask or camouflage, just the 'Man' walking by my side, I passed by all of them easily, and was literally invisible to them. They could not see me nor sense my presence, although they knew my identity and physical appearance, and were specifically out to get me.

I had complete sense of security as the 'Man' walked by my side, his arms on my shoulder

Once out of danger, the "Man' disappeared and I was safe in an open area. Then, while still in the dream, the verse below appeared in my mind.

John 8:59: "Then they took up stones to throw at Him; but Jesus hid Himself and went out of the temple, and going through the midst of them, and passed by."

I immediately woke up with a mixed feeling. It was one of exhaustion, as a man who had been on the run for a while, being pursued and on a wanted or hit list, and secondly with a sense of calm and peace, as I was saved by a man.

I knew at once in my spirit that that 'Man" in my dream was Jesus.

What is so special about this testimony?

I believe Jesus gave me that dream to give me a strong and deep reassurance that He will save us in difficult situations, even when my life was in danger, as He would be there to help me. The LORD went on to give me a second, equally powerful dream of His divine intervention, recounted below.

Testimony # 005   Jesus Saves me from a Beast

In my second dream, I was walking along a road to visit a 'Man'. While walking towards his house, and I was alone, I saw a big black animal, which appeared to like a huge dog about twenty feet in the distance, away from the path I was on.

A thought raced through my mind, that the animal may attack me. I had a sense of fear and concern. I was only a short distance from my destination, possibly less than 50 yards away, and I was hoping to make it there safely.

Almost in the next instance in this dream, I was literally engulfed by this beast like creature, with half of my body, from head to my waist in its mouth, with both my arms straight down on the side of my body; I was inside its huge mouth, well encircled by its jaw, with its very sharp teeth touching all around me and about to pierce into me at any moment, if I moved. I was very still, remaining quiet, helpless, not knowing what to do.

I knew that I was literally facing death as I froze physically, not daring to make the slightest movement, because the slightest movement would have killed me. I was not in pain, and though uncertain of my fate. It was a very real situation. Somehow, I was calm and not terrified, despite half of me physical being in the mouth and jaw of the beast.

Almost at once, the 'Man' I was visiting came out to rescue me. He stood about 12 feet from us, and then He spoke, and I could hear him clearly:

"Let him go!"

"LET him go!!"
"LET him GO!!"

He spoke with authority, and repeated His command three times steadily, progressively louder each time. He did not shout. It was an order that the beast had to follow and obey. I felt safe and had that assurance that freedom was imminent. Even though I knew would be delivered, I had to keep very still waiting for the beast to release me.

It remained stubborn and did not do so for about 30 seconds in my mental thought, which was a long time for me. During that time, I was still in great danger of being killed. I remained very still and strangely calm. And after thirty seconds, the jaw opened very slowly, and suddenly in an instance, I was out of the mouth, free and now standing beside the 'Man'.

The beast withdrew a short distance back. It stood still and appeared the same big black mass, as when I first saw it. I could not see any feature or the face. I took control at once, and was now staring at the beast, a dark black mass, about fifteen feet from me. Anger mixed with courage rose inside me, and this time it was me who declared with authority while speaking to the beast, increasing in my voice and tone each time.

"Show me your face."
"SHOW me your face."
"SHOW me your face."

I raised my voice a bit, and for the last sentence, I was bold and loud.

Suddenly, I was attacked again, but this time, only my left arm up to the forearm was inside the mouth of what appeared to be a feminine deity. I could see the face of an unfamiliar South Asian looking female deity.

Again, I was not afraid nor in pain while being attacked, and the Man was still by my side, observing everything I was doing. He did not intervene or said anything, but His mere Presence gave me boldness and authority.

I somehow had something sharp in my left hand, - a kind of blade. With it, I slit through the throat of the spirit deity, as it screamed and screamed and was then lifeless.

I was free and unharmed.

The dream ended there, and I woke up. It was so vivid, that my whole physical self was exhausted and tense, but there was a deep sense of relief that I was free. I was saved from death by a 'Man', who had intervened so timely.

I was now sitting up in bed, alert in the middle of the night. I knew in my heart at once that the Man was Jesus. I was going to His House to visit Jesus, symbolic of going to church for service.

This dream took place just before I went on a mission trip in India.

What are these two dreams telling?

There are dangers out there, as there is an adversary. Nevertheless, fear not for Jesus is our Protector and Defender, and He is with me and you throughout our journey on earth.

His help and protection are both timely. We in fact, have the authority to act as He is with us.

Testimony # 006   Messenger in the Fog

My medical school classmate in his mid-forties suffered a massive heart attack, and was rushed to hospital. These were the days before "Primary Coronary Intervention", where emergency insertion of a 'stent' to unblock the coronary arteries is a routine.

He was immediately rushed into the operation theater for an emergency bypass surgery. His heart had stopped for a total of four hours by the time the heart beat was restored after the bypass surgery. News of his sudden illness shocked the medical fraternity, especially his classmates.

Somehow, I had delayed visiting him till about two months into the admission. He was still in coma and was ventilated in the Intensive Care Unit of the National Heart Center of Kuala Lumpur, with kidney in a shutdown at that time.

Here was I visiting him at this critical period, about two months after the heart attack, while he was still on a ventilator, all alone with him in the room.

Peng (not his real name) was an easy-going beer drinking and cigarette smoking doctor, a qualified pathologist at that time. Religion and faith were not his pet topics up until then. If one were to share with him about Jesus at the time when he was well, he would probably laugh at us.

Seeing him in that state, I was both helpless and frank at his bedside. This was exactly what I said to him.

"Peng, you have no hope really. Your only hope is to cry out to Jesus for help. Just cry out to Jesus for help." I said a short and simple prayer of healing for him, and then left.

Little did I know what was happening to the soul trapped inside a perishing body. Apparently, he was truly in a desperate situation. It was dark and scary, and getting darker and darker. He was truly helpless and fearful, knowing that his life was critically in danger right at that moment, when suddenly, "he heard my familiar voice telling him to call upon Jesus."

There did not seem to be any other alternative. The fog was getting thicker and it was getting darker, and he did not know how to get out of it. So, in desperation and sheer fear, he followed my advice and started calling out to "Jesus" for help. He recalled later on, in his published testimony that he must have called on to the name of Jesus, over hundreds of time.

I came again about two weeks after that, and during this next visit, I met both the wife and their daughter. I found out then that she was a Methodist. I shared to them that I had prayed with him during the last visit, and that I had urged him to call upon the name of Jesus. I did not see any response, as there appeared before me a 'lifeless body'.

On this second visit, I spoke in a more joking and provocative way, and asked him why he wasn't waking up. This was exactly what I said:

"What's wrong with you! Why aren't you waking up? Do you want us to pump in some alcohol and nicotine into your drip?"

I paused and suddenly, I saw him smile, even with a tube (endotracheal tube) down his throat. That was a truly exciting sight, and the wife remarked that it was his first ever smile since he was ill. I left and did not visit him.

News soon got around that "Peng has shown remarkable progress, was extubated, breathing on his own and would soon be discharged."

My visit was sometime in October that year, perhaps in 1996 or 1997.

Peng, my dear friend and pathologist lived on for another good 21 years, working and practicing as a pathologist, with no evidence of brain damage. The National Heart Center remembers him as a 'miracle man', for his miraculous recovery against the odds.

About six months after my visit, he came back to work. Around that time, his recollections returned to that very moment when I challenged him. He wrote a testimony entitled: "The Messenger in the Fog" describing his conversion during coma.

Peng was a changed man after that. He was a regular church goer, and served as an usher for a season with his wife. He lived on for another 21 years, until a sudden acute illness took his physical life recently.

This testimony is true because I am that messenger in the fog. It has also changed my approach to comatose patients, and several more of these patients have responded to my conversations with them, as I now regularly talk to my comatose patients.

Truly, all glory and praise go to our God and Maker for His Name is awesome and powerful.

Ever since this experience, I have been sharing this simple principle:

"If ever or whenever in trouble, call out the Mighty Name of Jesus, and He will save you."

Testimony #001 continues to remind us that God is a timely prayer answering God. He is not slack or slow, as some think He is, nor is He deaf or blind to your cries and suffering. He hears and sees your distress calls and your plight. Jesus will surely save you.

Why is this testimony so powerful?

Peng a non-believer in coma heard my advice to all upon the Name of Jesus. He did so, many, many times, and woke up, recovered and worked again for just over two decades.

The comatose can hear. Never give up on them! Anyone can pray. A believer or non-believer calling upon the Name of Jesus is prayer.

Testimony # 007   Preaching to the Comatose

My dear beloved relative was admitted under my care.

She was suffering from a terminal cancer, and the cancer had spread to the liver, and it was the third day of coma.

Over the past four years, I was her nurse, administrating chemotherapeutic agents at home, as instructed by her oncologist. Now and then, I would share about our Lord. As the illness progressed, I sensed that time was running out.

I recall this particular situation, while I had set the line, and the chemotherapeutic agent was running when I directly said that "it would be good if you accept Jesus as your Savior and Lord."

She shouted back suddenly:

"No! I don't want. I don't want means I don't want! Even if Jesus is true, I still do not want Him!" she declared aloud.

I was stunned, shaken and upset. However, I respectfully replied as follows:

"Okay, okay, calm down, it's all right. I will still pray for you, and start a special 21 day fast for you, so that you can get well."

"It's up to you," she replied nonchalantly.

I began a 21-day Daniel fast specifically for this precious soul. Prior to that, I recalled having done a 40-day, dinner to dinner fast and had included this beloved dear relative in that season of fasting.

Lo and behold, as soon as my fast had ended, she lapsed into coma, as the tumor cells had already invaded the liver. I picked up the phone and dialed for an ambulance. Rushing into the washroom to get ready to accompany her, I wept before the LORD!

In tears, I cried, "Please LORD, please. Please do not let me lose this precious soul!"

I heard almost immediately an audible soft voice saying, "When you sow in tears, you will reap with joy!"

What a truly deep and timely assurance it was! (From Psalm 126:5) The ambulance arrived within 20 minutes and we took off to the General Hospital in Kuala Lumpur, the biggest hospital in the country, at that time, until now.

She was admitted to the Liver Unit under a renown hepatologist. On the third day, close to midnight, I bumped into the specialist and he told me frankly that there was no hope, as my dear relative was still in coma.

Her daughter insisted to me that we should still try to restore her conscious state even if it was just for a few weeks, urging me to take over the care. I made the proposition, and my colleague agreed for me to take over the care and transfer this relative to my ward, a neurology ward.

Then and there, at around midnight, with the help of nurses, we did a transfer of this precious soul to my care. On arrival in my ward, the family wished me 'Goodnight' and assumed naturally that I would be on night duty that night to accompany my dear beloved.

I was bright and alert at midnight, with adrenaline slow flowing high in my bloodstream. I was alone, the bedside 'nurse' on duty for this precious beloved, - just the two of us.

A great God-idea flashed into my mind.

"Preach to her!".

I placed a stethoscope with the hearing pieces to her ears, and I began to speak and preach the Good News about Jesus Christ directly into the receiver diaphragm of the stethoscope. It is very, very loud when we speak into a stethoscope, as it magnifies sound many times over.

The Good News of Jesus Christ reached the inner depths of her soul - loud and clear. I did this for about 20 minutes.

Suddenly, to my surprise, she woke up, opened her eyes widely, and looked at me straight in the face and spoke. I was obviously delighted that she had woken up after three days of coma.

I said, "So wonderful! You have woken up! You were in coma for three days!"

"Nonsense," she said, totally oblivious of the three days in coma, and denying her previous state.

"It's true. Can I give you some water?" I said, and stretched out a small teaspoon of water for her, knowing that her throat would be dry.

She closed her mouth and, in an instance, spit at my face.

Wow, that's strange, I thought. Why would anyone do that? One's throat would have been dry after three days of unconsciousness. Who would reject an act of kindness? I continued to test, spoon by spoon up to about six times, and received six small splashes of spit on my face.

(I have testified the analogy of someone just struggling out of a desert, thirsty and dehydrated, and here comes along a good and kind Samaritan offering water, but is rejected rudely.)

Then, she spoke, "I will report you to the police tomorrow."

I kept my cool, and retreated and we dosed off for the night, with barely a few hours left for the night. Both the sick and caregiver rested.

In the morning, as expected, she did just that – complain to the next of kin, that this 'man was sharing to me about Jesus.'

The immediate family, though delighted that their beloved had awoken from coma, then put a cordon around her and turned on some chanting music. I was warned clearly not to share any more 'Christian stuff' or else! They had accepted that death was imminent, and this was the final days. In fact, there was perfect peace around her, as she planned her departure, distributing her jewelry to the children, and giving instructions to each, planning some details of her own funeral, including her wish to wear a white silk gown for her final resting dress.

(What a coincidental choice, indeed so far, the first and only time I have experienced a Chinese male or female dressed in silk white gown as a final resting attire, not even a Christian! It was so angelic and appropriate, as the story would show.)

Somehow, I knew that I would have another chance, though the window of opportunity was narrow. I had to tread cautiously. It had to be a brief moment when she could respond with a clear 'yes', yet not strong enough to protest should any of my attempts fail.

God has a perfect timing! What a coincidence it was that my dad was admitted with a major stroke in the next bed, and both dear beloveds were now under my personal care. My step-mother, who is an intercessor and prayer warrior, was visiting my dad, when I urged her to go over to pray for this precious unsaved soul.

I accompanied her to visit this beloved unsaved, who was in the next room. Step mother was warmly received, as they extended courteous greetings, smiled and were very polite. It was then, that my step-mother asked for permission to say a short prayer. This beloved relative agreed and accepted to be prayed for!

It was a beautiful prayer as I recall, as my step-mum prayed that the love of Jesus come, fill, overflow and heal. I have been praying for this precious soul and family for over a decade, and this was the first time, a family member had agreed to be prayed for, what more in the final days of her life.

The clock was ticking, as days went by. Time was running out, but each day had been peaceful, free of pain, and I remained in the outer circle, waiting anxiously for my opportunity to come again. By this time, drowsiness was about to set in, and eyes remained close mostly.

One evening, perhaps about ten days after that special prayer, I heard clearly, "He who calls upon my Name will be saved!" It echoed in my heart, and I knew that it was a word of reassurance from Heaven for this precious soul. But, when?

The window of opportunity fell on the next day. I had seen all my patients, including the two 'oldies', completed my work for the day, and had driven off. I was barely, half a mile from my hospital, heading towards home, when I heard, "Turn back now; turn back now."

In obedience, I turned back and headed straight to the room where this precious soul was in. I ask two of my dear relatives, "What happened?"

She had poo-pooed and the nurses were changing her. I asked whether they had eaten, to which they replied negative. I urged them to go for dinner, while I stood by.

Since she had regained consciousness, she was never alone, and the family made certain that she was never left alone with me! I told my nurses to clean her up quickly, which they did. They had led their guards down. That gave me a good 20 to 30 minutes window of opportunity, which had hitherto been shut by a round the clock blockade, that was ensuring I was not alone 'to do my tricks again.'

I turned off the tape recorder that was playing continuous chanting. I then spoke and asked very calmly,

"My dear beloved, this is the last opportunity, the last chance for you to call upon Jesus. Will you please call Jesus, please?"

I pleaded again, as she could hear, but with eyes closed. I paused, look intently into her face, and then 'Bingo'! she moved her lips and said: "Yes."

"Please call the Name of Jesus," I repeated. "Okay" was the reply, and I asked again and she repeated, five times in all.

My beloved had accepted Jesus Christ as her Savior. Wow! Hallelujah! Praise the LORD! She made it. She called upon the Name of the LORD. She had confirmed it five times, in our local dialect, Hokkien. She had finally said "Yes" to Jesus!

The next day, I wanted confirmation and placed a fleece, that this beloved would open her eyes and show me again. I was right by her side, and for a brief moment, she had opened her eyes and stared right into me, when I asked: "Do you have peace now?"

She replied with a clear nod, with eyes open, and then closed her eyes. It was to be the last time her eyes opened. The next day, or second day after her calling upon Jesus, I decided not to do my rounds, and just sit by her bedside, sensing that time was limited. Two of my relatives had decided to go out to look for a casket. That left me with one other relative. Her phone rang, and she went out to take the call.

It was in those few seconds, when I was all alone that it happened. I turn to look at the beloved and suddenly, she turned her neck and breathed her last. I was alone with her in those final seconds, as I prayed that her soul belonged to Jesus. There was perfect peace. One soul was ushered into the Kingdom of Heaven.

As the doctor, I certified death and life, as the last certificate to the National Archives, was recorded: "Christian". Hallelujah! Praise the LORD!

What did I learn from this testimony?

It was a tough, tough one. And, I was the one, the only one that could and did stand in the gap to intercede and battle for this beloved soul. Often, you too, are the only one who is in that position to make the difference, to intercede, to stand in the gap.

Will you do so?

Testimony # 008   Near Miss with Fire Engine

It was one of those busy mid-week, mid-day traffic jams, typically after a Friday noon time prayer hour. I was in between hospitals and was approaching a normally easy round-a-bout, when it was a grid-lock situation with cars crawling into and out of the round-a-bout.

It took me about ten minutes to just enter the round-a-bout with great effort, and my thoughts were "if only I could clear half of the circle", I would be able to zoom off to my next destination. I had to literally inch my way along the circle, holding my breath, as Christians practice never to swear or curse, especially along the road.

I had entered the round-a-bout, which was a great achievement, and moved barely a quarter of a circle, having to go straight onward, when suddenly, I was delighted to see the car in front of me literally zooming off. It left me with a clear path and completely free access to do the same and get going.

Just when I was about to press the accelerator, as one would normally do in such a situation, after having waited, crawled and lingered in an unusually long traffic jam, I heard a distant soft ringing of bells.

This distant soft 'bell' ringing, was not quite that of an ambulance, and more like an ice-cream vendor in search of kids looking for a treat.

Something inside me, 'a still small voice', told me to pause and look left, which I did. To my shock and horror, I saw a fire-engine dashing right across my path, exactly where I would have been if I had pressed the accelerator. It would have been a sure direct collision with a heavy fire-engine impacting my car right in the middle on the passenger's side.

I took a deep breath and thanked God for the near miss, and drove on!

My recurring thoughts for the next hour was that, "if I had stepped up my speed and ignored the strange bell ringing sound, I would have suffered a direct collision." Who knows what would have happened, and the testimony would have been very different?

I thank God for this, and many near misses in my life and yours. I thank my unseen angels for their hand in nudging me to "pause and look left."

What have I learned from this testimony?

We could have died many times. I can recall some near-death situations, about eight so far in my life. Admittedly, some near misses are due to our own carelessness, like driving and speaking, reading and writing on our so-called smartphones.

Testimony # 009   Encounter with Angels

I have not had the privilege of seeing angels yet. Some of the people I know can see things in the spiritual realm. Here are some testimonies.

I met a patient who regularly sees the unseen realm, and had his own encounters with his angels.

He was apparently quite ill on one occasion, when two men sat down beside him, one on each side. He asked them who they were. They introduced themselves as his angels, and even told him their names, which sounded Greek to me. This same brother was talking to me on the hospital corridors, when he told me that he had just seen my two angels, and was chatting with them.

They spoke to him about me. What they told him has been an edification to me since, as my angels described me to him. He said, "Your angels said to me, that you are a man of pure heart and clean hands."

I immediately responded in humility and said, "LORD, may I have a pure mind and a clean tongue too."

My sister-in-law Lydia was a young Christian, probably of about several weeks of age, when she experienced a period of confusion. She had come from a background of Buddhism/Taoism to Christianity. Wonderfully, she gave her life to Jesus on Christmas day.

She was performing some household chores, when suddenly, an angel appeared before her. The angel sat down beside her and talked to her for about twenty minutes, encouraged her on in her new found faith. His appearance was that of a middle eastern Caucasian, according to her. Lydia said that she knew that he was an angel, and not Jesus.

Just before leaving, the angel told her to read Hebrews 4;2. He held up a small scroll with the words, Hebrews 4:2 on it. As she was a young Christian, she had to check up what Hebrews 4:2 said.

Hebrews 4:2 says, "For indeed the gospel was preached to us as well as to them; but the Word which they heard did not profit them, not being mixed with faith in those who heard it."

Then, the angel left.

I heard this testimony some years ago, and read the verse many times after that, and it was only about a year ago, that the powerful revelation of the word impacted me.

Paraphrased, it means that God has already made available so many rich blessings, as He has promised, and that unless it is mixed and received with faith, we can literally miss out on the blessings of God.

What have I learned from this testimony?

Figuratively, it means that if there is a truck giving free goodies passing by us every day, it

is for us to believe and to go out and receive the goodies, whether food, cash or blessings. If we doubt, and do not want to hear, see or act on it, we will receive nothing.

Testimony # 010   Team Work in Deliverance

Mr Rajoo was a retired school teacher. He fell ill and was admitted to a public hospital and was very sick and near death. His family was informed that he would not make it and the doctor suggested that he be taken home.

Rajoo's brother was a pastor in Malacca. He came and prayed fervently for his healing, and following that, Rajoo began to respond. At this point, the pastor brother suggested that he be transferred to my hospital to be under my care. That was the first intervention. Death was deferred.

I was the second link in his amazing story of deliverance.

On arrival in my ward, I found a man, awake but blankly staring, with occasional words spoken on and off. He appeared unfriendly and confrontational. He expressed his dislike for me when I entered his room, giving me a deep 'deadly' stare.

I recall entering his room as his doctor, and facing a hostile patient, who was even swearing at me. Knowing that he was from a Christian background, and with his wife's permission, I went directly to his side and said that I would pray for his recovery, confirming that he had recovered from the first phase of his illness. I said literally that I was going to pray to Jesus for his full recovery. He objected immediately and said, "No! Pray in the name of satan!"

This went on for about a week plus, during which he also threatened to kill his wife. He would also be chanting all sorts of chants meant for funerals. The spirit of death was very strong around him.

I recall that by God's grace breakthrough came and he managed to call the Name of the LORD, within a few days. I however felt that he needed to be ministered to further.

At this stage, I met a Pastor James Doss on the corridor and invited him to minister salvation and the Word of God to this man, following his deliverance. By God's grace. He came to believe and receive Jesus as his Lord and Savior (again). He was well enough to go home within a few days after that.

On discharge from hospital, I connected him to Pastors Joseph and Lily Selva to continue to uphold them, and support them in prayer. They visited and ministered to him, and he fully recovered.

All in all, it was four stages, involving four men of God, the first who battled for his life, the second who intervened for his deliverance, and the third who ministered salvation, and the fourth who secured his faith in the Lord.

About a year after the whole episode, he walked into my office and gave a RM 2,000 love offering for the "work of God." Although a pensioner with limited funds, he and his wife insisted that this was money he had set aside for God's Work.

What did I learn from this testimony?

Team effort is important for battles to be won.
All of us are able to play a role in the marketplace ministry, and be a part of God's
wonderful machinery of ministry.

Testimony # 011   Seven Consecutive Witnesses

Ms Tan (not her real name) was a medical representative for a pharmaceutical company. They regularly drop by to promote and discuss the drugs and medications from their companies. It was about 5 p.m. and the clinic had just closed, when I saw her waiting outside my consultation room while I was practicing in Kuala Lumpur Hospital. As a practice, I very seldom reject any sales person, without enquiring what they wanted. Even if I am in a hurry, I would usually hear them out at least for a minute.

I told her that the office was already closed and perhaps, we could talk outside. Just as I was about to sit down beside her, I heard a still small voice say, "Share with her." I thought, it meant having fellowship with her.

After saying hello and sitting down, I asked her immediately, "Are you a Christian?" to which she immediately replied "No, I am a Buddhist."

I felt taken aback as I had clearly heard the prompting to talk to her about her faith, and the answer was a clear negative.

"Oh, do you mind if I shared the Gospel with you?" I continued, in obedience to the prompting I received.

She replied, "No, I do not mind."

I shared very shortly in 10-15 minutes about Jesus, as Savior of the world and that through Him; we can enter into eternal life. With that, I asked her to proceed to share about her products. She did so, and then she left.

Over the next two weeks, she experienced a series of strange meetings, where another six people did the same thing to her. They shared the Gospel to her, one after the other, in six different occasions and locations.

She had a meeting with an Indian lady doctor in another hospital, and after that brief discussion, Ms Tan asked her, "Doctor, I have been talking mostly. Why don't you tell me about your day and yourself?"

The lady doctor said, "You know, the most wonderful thing in my life is that Jesus is my Lord and Savior." Ms Tan was surprised and stunned.

On another occasion, she was sitting in a clinic, waiting for her opportunity to see a doctor, when a woman beside her was reading a Bible. They made eye contact, and the next thing was the woman began to share about Jesus.

In another clinic, she had waited patiently to meet the doctor and it was already 1 p.m. The doctor came out and said, "I am sorry; I cannot talk to you. We are having a lunch fellowship. Why not you join us?" She invited her in to join her first Full Gospel Businessman's lunch hour fellowship gathering.

After the seventh such encounter being witnessed to seven times consecutively in two weeks, including mine, she walked into my office dazed and told me this.

"Doc, something is happening to me. Since the day you talked to me about Jesus, another six persons have shared with me too."

I was delighted to hear that and told her, "Well, The LORD is sending you all these messengers to tell you." Even after that seventh encounter with saint after saint, I did not push her to accept Jesus then and there.

She left and did a "Christian thing", without knowing that it was so. She put a fleece before God!

She said, "Almighty God, show me a sign by next Wednesday noon time, and I will believe and accept Jesus as my Lord and Savior."

Just before noon on that day, her phone rang. This was in the days before the mobile phone were a common accessory. She walked over and picked up the phone and heard a very familiar voice. It was her college mate, whom she had not heard from for years. He was a Christian and she recalled having had quite a few sharp disagreements and differences when they had talked about faith. This same guy was on the phone.

This was the exact question that she asked Alan (not his real name), and his reply.

"Alan! Can I ask you one question before you speak? Have you been praying for me?"

Alan answered, "Yes, almost every day!"

She believed in Jesus at that instant. They met up and started attending church together.

I do not have the end of the story yet, as to whether they lived happily ever after. I sensed strongly that this young man was pursuing Ms Tan but knew that she was not a believer, thus never made the move. He instead prayed fervently to the LORD for her salvation. Our Master arranged for seven people, including and beginning with 'yours truly' to share the Gospel to her. What an amazing master plan of His!

I somehow sense that they would have ended up together, but at the time of writing, am unable to confirm this.

What I learned from this testimony?

God is a Master Planner. Keep praying for a beloved and in His time, the fruit will be ripe and ready.

Everyone also needs to sow and share. How can they know if they do not hear, and how can they hear if no one tells them? [Romans 10]

Testimony # 012   Adrift in Pacific Ocean

I was snorkelling off the Green Island, near Cairns during one of my medical seminars, when I was miraculously saved from drowning in the Pacific Ocean.

We took off from Cairns in a ship to the island, and from where the ship docked, we walked along the long pier to the beach front. It was a medium size group, and we were sent off in pairs as buddies, all equipped with snorkelling gear and a pair of flippers. There was no briefing, apart from us being told to be back in two hours.

So, off we went me with my buddy whom I had just met. There were hundreds of tourists on the beach swimming and snorkelling away happily in the great and bright sunny day. I recall that as the ship was approaching the island and again when I was walking along the pier, I heard a still small voice distinctly cautioning me, with just two words, "Be careful; be careful." I took little notice of that, not knowing what it had meant then.

So, there was I a novice in the sea, hardly a swimmer, with little snorkelling experience since a trip to the East Coast Island of Redang in Malaysia, about to plunge into the largest ocean in the world. I had barely been out about five minutes in the shallow waters when I felt that the flippers were heavy and clumsy, and I turned back to put the flippers back on the beach, covered by my towel and a small carrier bag.

Off I went again, this time heading towards an area where the corals were best seen. The guide had told us that we had to swim out to where our boat or ship was docked, and that was quite a distance off.

I probably took 20 minutes of my mental time to get to where they had said was best to view the corals. I was disappointed and muttered to myself that this was nothing compared to Redang. I am not an adventurous person by nature. Nevertheless, I decided to swim further out to see more. Little did I know that I was swimming along the currents that were sweeping me directly towards the vast Pacific Ocean. There was a protective wooden barrier built into the sea to reduce the impact of the currents, and the site where I was originally had been was near the end of that protection. I innocently swam out for another 20 minutes, assisted by the sweeping currents, when I decided to look back. I was probably out for a good 50 minutes by then.

To my horror, all I saw was a line showing the beach in a distance with no signs of human life! I was all alone in the vast ocean. It was quite a frightening feeling. All I could do was gasp an equivalent of "Oh, my God!!"

I vividly recall that it was a frightening and sinking feeling, and I had no time to think or pray, as the fear of death sank deep into me.

[Here was I, all alone in the Pacific Ocean, and all I saw was a line in the distance. In such states of panic, as many will testify, there is no time to think, pray or say anything.]

I put my head down in the water with my snorkel, and no flippers and swam the fastest Olympic breaking stretch in my life. I am convinced that I broke a distance record of the Olympics, because in my 'mental time' of one minute, I was on the beach with legs beside me! I had arrived on the shallow part of the beach, as legs were beside me. I stood up, not even recalling whether I thanked God. At that same instance, leg cramps seized me.

I was safe, saved by my angels who must have pushed me in one minute, over a distance that took me 40-50 minutes to cover going out.

When I flew back the next day from Cairns, the plane had passed the island and I saw exactly the situation I was in. I was swimming along the same direction as the fast currents, and went past beyond the area where the waves were blocked by a wooden barrier.

Wow, I could have died, if not for some miracle that "pushed me back to shore" in one minute. I checked the estimated distance on Google Maps, as it was about 200 meters from beach to where the ship is docked, and it was another 200-300 meters that I drifted away, hence a total of between 400-500 meters. Either way the world record runs between 3.4 to 4.08 minutes respectively for 400 and 500 meters.

A year later, back in Malaysia, I read in the papers that a famous politician had drowned in the same area.

Recently, on another trip in Langkawi, Malaysia, when the boat was near the shore and people were visible on the beach and the waves prevented the ship from docking, we were given the option to swim to shore. I did so. It took me a good ten minutes to reach the shore for that very much shorter distance.

What did I learn from this testimony?

It was a close shave for me, and my time was not up yet.
Our angels, yours and mine are always at hand to save up and protect us, and I have no doubt at all that I broke the 400-meter swimming record, shaving it by at least two minutes.

Testimony # 013   The Unwilling Witness – Lesson One

It was one Monday morning, when I felt tired, exhausted and having been active in sharing the Gospel, I told the Lord Jesus this, as I was driving to work.

"Lord, I am exhausted today; do I have to share the Gospel today?"

I literally told my Lord and Savior Jesus Christ that I was not 'willing' to share the Good News that day, as I was tired.

That was the beginning of a personal lesson, stretched over two days, and a demonstration of His Majestic Hand and Power over that period, as the Master clearly showed the ease through the working of the Holy Spirit, which is the Spirit of God.

Over the next three hours, through this unwilling servant and witness, a tired son who wanted to rest for that day, five precious souls were ushered into the Kingdom of God. After I had made that confession that I had no intention to share the Gospel that day, God intervened and used me to bring 5 souls into the Kingdom of God. How did He do it? How did it happen?

On the wall of my clinic is a plaque displaying the "Fruits of the Spirit", and each fruit is displayed in vertical order i.e. love, joy, peace, longsuffering, kindness, goodness, faithfulness, gentleness, and self control. [Galatians 5:22]

A couple brought their elderly parents to see me. They had been serving in Beijing, as marketplace laborers for Jesus. I was busy checking the father, when the daughter-in-law Jean stopped me and said, "Please share the Good News to my father-in-law."

"Oh, okay," I replied, a little surprised, and proceeded to talk about Jesus, the Savior for mankind, and the need to invite Him into our lives. I invited the elderly man to do so.

He listened, paused and then nodded his agreement.

"Can we pray now to welcome Jesus into our life?" I asked. He said yes.

I then guided him to say the sinner's prayers aloud, with wife, son and same daughter-in-law listening on. I was so pleased, and my spirit was lifted up. I proceeded to complete the medical examination, when Jean interrupted me again and asked me to next lead her mother-in-law to the faith in Christ.

I said in Hokkien, a Chinese dialect, "Auntie, your husband has become a Christian. It would be good if you too followed and joined him in believing Jesus. How about it?"

She had witnessed everything, and she was not slow or confused. Instead, she surprised me with a clear affirmative answer. So, we proceeded again in Hokkien and she personally declared her belief in Jesus Christ, and invited Him as her Savior into her life.

As soon as she had said 'Amen', she asked, ""What should we do with our idols?", thus confirming that she knew the commitment of her new faith.

Both I and her son assured her that they will know what to do with it.

Then, there was another case, and another case and another, totalling five wonderful ones ushered into the Kingdom of God. Each one was a simple straightforward situation. All that I needed was a cue, e.g. a cross worn by an accompanying relative, and I was able to ask the patient whether she was a Christian. The relative wearing the cross would then tell me to share with her mother, or husband or wife, and one by one agreed to invite Jesus into her life.

I looked up at the clock on the wall and it was 1 p.m. I was stunned and overjoyed that on a busy working day in barely three hours, The LORD had used an 'unwilling witness' to bring five souls into His Kingdom.

Is it a big deal? Yes, indeed, and for two reasons for me. Firstly, every single soul is precious and when one soul is saved, there is a big celebration in heaven. It is surely a miracle for one soul to come to Christ, considering how tough it is for some people to believe.

Secondly, despite a lot of effort, this humble servant had never led more than three people to Christ in a single day, one-to-one up until then. Five was the record, and it had happened on a day when I was tired and not willing.

Lesson 2 would continue the next working day.

What did I learn from this?

May this lesson be yours as it is mine too, that it is His Mighty Hand, and the Holy Spirit of God who moves hearts to believe and receive Jesus as Savior, no matter how eloquent or persuasive we are. All credit and glory go to God.

Apart from Jesus, we can do nothing. If thus I boast that I have been used by God to touch over 500 souls, or if I declare that I have led that number to Christ, it is to say that "God has used this humble vessel" to touch many lives so that Christ Jesus is made known to them. [John 15:5]

I no longer count or add on to total how many souls I have won for the Kingdom, because it is GOD, through His Son and the working of the Holy Spirit that wins souls for the Kingdom, when we submit to Him as willing (or even unwilling) vessels.

Testimony # 014   Declaring a Great Harvest – Lesson Two

This happened the following day, the day after the LORD ushered in five precious souls, on a day when I was an "unwilling witness."

I woke up in the morning fully charged up, excited to serve the LORD, and in a complete upswing, opposite to and unlike the day before.

I picked up my Nokia phone (this was in the days before WhatsApp) and texted to a few friends excitedly, declaring that:

 "Today is a great day of harvest for the LORD. Hallelujah!"

That was exactly what I texted, and sent out to just a few special friends and ministers, namely Brothers Tek Seng, Tuan Soon and Pastor Jason. I then went to work just like the day before, except that on this day, this humble servant was willing and keen to share the Gospel to save souls.

It was a busy morning, and I was working continuously when I glanced at the clock on my wall. It was already 1 p.m. and not one single soul had been saved! I continued to work throughout the afternoon non-stop, and it was 'suddenly' 5.30 p.m. I proceeded to a Hospital Doctors meeting at Gleneagles Hospital, and when the meeting ended, I realised it was already 7.30 p.m.

As I rushed out to the wards to do my evening ward rounds for the day, I remembered that I had earlier posted in the morning that it would be "a great day of harvest for the LORD". However, it was nearly the end of the working day, not one soul was saved yet, through me!

Was it my own lofty imagination? Was it my own ego to declare a great day of harvest? Those were my thoughts. Nevertheless, I then decided to try to win some souls in the ward. Shifting gear towards 'arm-twisting', I urged one middle-aged lady to receive Jesus as her Savior.

She responded and said the sinner's prayer. What a relief, I thought. One soul saved for the Kingdom! But then, "one is not great" as I had texted. I delayed texting that one soul had been saved to the same group of friends.

It was about 8.15 p.m. in the night, as I was passing by the Intensive Care Unit (ICU), when the Master showed His Mighty Hand, in that last hour.

There was a crowd of about eleven people outside the ICU, and their mother was critically ill and about to pass on. She was a believer together with one son, and only a few hours ago, she had been declared 'Brain Dead' and had even showed a sign when she raised her left arm and placed it on her chest.

I greeted the crowd of eleven people, among who was a son who was a believer. The spirit of boldness rose up in me, as I addressed them, telling them that this was the last hour for her mother. I then said this:

"I know that you are grieving as your mother is about to leave us. However, we are comforted and assured that she will be in Heaven with God. I believe that it is a good time for the whole family to come to receive Jesus Christ as your Savior. Would all of you follow me as we pray to invite Jesus into your lives?

I looked all around and I could see all heads nodding in agreement. Then and there, I said a simple prayer of conviction that Jesus is Lord and Savior, accepting and welcoming of Jesus into our lives, what we often refer to as the 'sinner's prayer'.

Hallelujah and Praise the LORD! At that eleventh hour, at around 8.30 p.m. in the night, another ten souls were saved, making it a total of eleven souls saved on that day, "a great harvest of souls" for that day indeed.

The Holy Spirit had moved mightily at that last hour, using this humble servant to usher in a 'great harvest' for the Kingdom of God, for one family.

I immediately called Pastor Sophia of a nearby church and urged her to come to minister to the family. She replied that she would be there the next morning.

"No, Pastor, please come tonight. They need you."

Pastor Sophia came and ministered to the whole family, and went on later to conduct the funeral services for the family.

What can I say? What did I learn from these two lessons?

THE LORD had demonstrated His Mighty Hand in two lessons on two consecutive days; the first was an unwilling witness, and He still used me, and the second was the same, but now with a willing witness, when He showed up majestically at the final hour. Ultimately, it is all in God's Hand, and all things are possible with God.

Testimony # 015   Answered Prayer for Car Parks

Almost every Christian would have testimonies of answered prayer for car parks.

I will relate a few interesting ones. Before doing so, the answered prayers for car parks is a strong confirmation that God answers our prayers, and that His answers are timely and instant. God will never say, "Okay, come back at midnight and I will have a few car parks for you!" You need it now, and He grants it to you now.

I recall one instant when I told the LORD, "LORD, I will not trouble you today for a car park." I was visiting my dad and it was not easy to get a car park around where he lived. As soon as I said that, I could hear a soft gentle voice (ABBA, of course) say, "Son, it is never too much trouble to ask from Me."

Testimony # 1: London.

I had already driven around the block twice and I could not find a place to park. This was in 1985. I prayed, "LORD, I know you can provide for me a car park." Within a short distance, I found two empty places for me, not one but two, in the middle of the city on a midday!

Testimony # 2: With my sons.

I was out with my two sons, in their early teens, heading towards TGIF restaurant for dinner. I confidently declared to them that the LORD would provide a car park for us. It wasn't easy, as the place was busy and packed, on that Friday evening.

I had just passed by a car, and it reversed out of the box. It seemed like I had missed one good opportunity, yet I never doubted that God would provide. Next, closer to the restaurant, I saw a slot and contemplated whether I should park there, but it was not a legal place to park.

By now, we had reached the restaurant and all slots were occupied as my eyes could see. I saw a lady entering a car behind us. I quickly got out, and tapped on her window. She was surprised to have someone tap on her window, but still opened her windows. I then whispered to her to wait for me to reverse behind her, so that I could park there. She kindly cooperated and I parked there, right in front of the restaurant. My kids were touched as they saw God answer our prayers.

Testimony # 3: With my wife.

I was entering a garden park, where there was landscape exhibition going on, and there were hundreds of cars going around and round, literally meaning that a couple of hundreds of cars were looking for a few isolated spots. Where, when and how? It had to be when one car was moving out, and my car was just behind that driver that would have let me into that slot, as every car was crawling at pedestrian speed.

I told the wife, that with God all things were possible, and made this prayer, "Father your daughter (my wife) needs a car park." Within seconds, a few yards further, the car just beside and in front of ours, on the left moved, and we parked right there. What was the probability?

I know for sure that it was our Father in Heaven granting me the car park, because we asked.

Testimony # 4: Guided by Holy Spirit.

Once in a multilevel car park, many years back, when there was no indication where an empty slot was, I asked the Holy Spirit for directions. I heard "turn right now", and I followed and drove on, and a short distance after, I heard "turn left now", and I did so, and went on further until I heard again, "turn left now", and there a few slots from where I turned was an empty slot.

If it was on my own effort, I would have gone a few rounds before I would have found an empty slot, and who knows, someone else would have got there first. I know it was the Holy Spirit who guided me directly to that empty slot.

What did I learn from this testimony?

God is faithful and timely in answering our prayers when we ask and believe.
He did not delay in answering our prayers for a car park, because we need it then and there, not at midnight or the next day! Only believe.

Testimony # 016　Car Sold for Cash in A Day

This was in the United Kingdom in 1985, where I was studying and working briefly for my specialty training in Neurology.

I had bought a second hand Datsun Sunny for 1300 sterling pounds. I recall that I had bought it without thoroughly checking it, as its body was rusty. My brother-in-law had made a joke out of it, that it was not a good buy.

The car served me and my small family faithfully for a year, as we travelled around the UK during that time, with perhaps only a couple of breakdowns, all of which were assisted by the Automobile Association of UK (affiliated to the Malaysian AA).

I had completed my training and was about to leave for Malaysia. For the first time in my life, I did a DIY for the car as some rust had broken through a small part of the car. It was during the mid-autumn period. I had patched up the small hole, and sprayed over the area, and the car was ready for sale. I decided to put a small advert for one day, and it would appear the very next day.

My prayer was, "LORD, please let me sell it off quickly, and just one prospective interested buyer."

I was not keen to wait day after day, or to let buyer after buyer to view the car. The next day, I received a call, and the first interested customer took the car with me for a drive, and within half an hour agreed to buy it, and paid me cash 1000 pounds!

Just before the transaction, I informed him honestly that the car was rusty. He said, "It's okay."

Guess what business he was in? He operated a driving school!

What did I learn from this testimony?

God is so gracious and faithful to His beloved. He gave me favor.
I am my beloved and my beloved is mine. [Songs 6:3]

Testimony # 017   God's Hand is Not Short

It was a tight season financially.

In this marketplace ministry, which I know that I am in for over two decades now, one of the functions of our little group of donors, was generous giving and supporting of ministries and itinerant ministers. The need for support is always there, or in one word "endless".

I believe because one is involved and engaged in God's Work, and God is working through you and I, through a 'surrendered vessel', then we will continuously see these miracles of His Mighty Provision.

As mentioned, it was a tight season, and I could not help freely. A request had come from India and another from Dili, Indonesia, and one more from Sarawak. Also, a minister was expecting his first child, and I casually asked him where the baby would be delivered, and his answer told me of his need, as he said, "We are not sure yet.", even though the baby was due within a couple of months.

It was at this time that I called a dear friend Jonathan, about this dilemma and the great needs around us. Jonathan himself had been in this ministry of giving and helping and his words truly put me back on the right footing.

He said, "Tim, this is not your problem. It is the LORD's and His Hand is not short."

I used that verse immediately and texted to the several requests, assuring each one that God's Hand is not short and He will provide.

A lady walked into my office and requested a letter to assist her husband to travel for treatment in China. At that time, and even now, many patients travel abroad to seek alternative or complimentary treatment to China and India. This lady's husband's passport had been barred by Immigration for some reason which she or he did not tell me. However, on medical grounds, they would allow a temporary one-time travel.

My letter was correct and relevant, as he had an incurable condition. As soon I passed her the letter, she placed a wad of one hundred ringgit (Malaysian dollars) on the table and said, "Thank you Doctor, this is for you."

I immediately replied that I could not take it, as it was only a letter that I wrote. She expressed gratefulness to me, and insisted that I accepted the money.

I relented and replied, "All right then, but I will give it to charity."

It was ten thousand ringgit, an equivalent of nearly USD 3,000 then. I gave it all to the different needs above; the evangelist in Dili could renew his visa, while the pastor in India could pay for his son's fees, a man of God in Sarawak was blessed, and the minister was able to deliver his first child in the private hospital I was working in.

Hallelujah! Praise the LORD!

Behold, God's Hand is not short, that He cannot help. [Isaiah 59:1]

What have I learned from this testimony?

Exactly as the title states in Isaiah 59:1, that the LORD's Hand is not shortened that He cannot help. The LORD can help and He is willing.

Testimony # 018   God's Heavenly Cheque

This is a yet another testimony of God's provision and that His Hand is not shortened.

I was about to leave for a short mission trip in India, when I felt burdened to bring a blessing to the church I was visiting. Prince of Peace Ministries in Chennai was started by Bishop James Santhosam, and over three decades then, some 350 village churches have been formed. The needs were always there.

I told the LORD, "Surely, you must send me some funds. I cannot possibly be using my own funds for this trip."

That was exactly what I said that morning. I did not call anyone or ask anyone. At around noon, as I was walking along the corridors of the hospital, a man ran towards me and passed me an envelope. It was a cheque for 10,000 ringgit in Malaysian currency under my name.

I was delighted and thankful for God for His Provision and answered prayers. I went to the bank in the afternoon and requested for a demand Bank Draft for the same amount written out to the beneficiary.

When I went to collect the draft, the manager came out to tell me that it was an amazing figure, when converted to Indian rupees. He himself, a religious man of another faith said that it was a very special number, and must be God given.

The cheque came out in Indian rupees to be exactly, Rs 121,212.12 or **"12 12 12 12"**!

As I held the cheque in my hands with much gratitude, I heard a small voice say:

"This is my cheque. This is from my Government."

I was reminded that there is a Kingdom of Heaven. This fund had arrived from the Bank of Heaven, and it was confirmed by the amazing amount and figures that was displayed. There were four '12s' there in a row, and "12" is God's Kingdom number.

Then and there I heard.

"Twelve denotes the Kingdom of God"

There are twelve disciples, twelve tribes and twelve is the complete number, as God has chosen every number from one to twelve for a specific purpose.

I could hear in my mind, "One is the Unity of God, two is partnership in agreement, three is the Triune God, and a knot that cannot be broken, four denotes the cycle and seasons, and latitudes, five is about provision, blessings and ministry e.g. five loaves, five-fold ministry, six is the length of work before rest, and seven is the full week, while eight, nine and ten, eleven all have meanings."

Then and there I understood why the enemy chose 13, because God had hallowed all the first 12 numbers and the adversary chose the next one and made it 'unlucky'.

Numbers is not necessarily all superstition. God is a God of numbers, and there is significance in numbers.

What did I learn from this testimony?

I was amazed at God's timeliness in His Provision, and answered prayers. The LORD provides and His Hand is not short. I learned that God has given significance to numbers.

Testimony # 019   The Cup overflows

Surely goodness and mercy follow us all the days of our lives.

This testimony is about a senior pastor who has served the LORD faithfully with his wife for over 25 years. He came to see me for headaches. I did a brain scan for him, and discovered that he was suffering from a large brain tumor. It was a benign or non-cancerous tumor called 'Meningioma', and it had been growing between the skull and the brain for many years.

I asked him whether he wanted the surgery at the private hospital I was working in, or that it be done in a public hospital where it would be much cheaper. He said he would pray and let me know in a week.

The following week, Pastor Johnny (not his real name) came with his wife and expressed his wish to have the operation at my hospital.

"Great!" I replied. "I will get you a good neurosurgeon. Let us pray for God's provision. Also, do you mind writing a short note about yourself, so that I can use it to raise some funds?"

He wrote a short note, and then we prayed. As we were praying, there was a knock on my clinic door, and a man delivered a cheque to me for RM 30,000, to be used for the Kingdom of God. I was surprised, and because of the timeliness of the arrival of the cheque, I said, "I believe these funds are for you."

Over the next week, we raised another RM20,000 and at the same time, the church where Pastor Johnny was serving in gave a RM15,000 cheque in support, thus totaling RM65,000 for the surgery and treatment. Crowd funding had not yet been around at that time, but the LORD provides.

The operation was successfully carried out and the bill came to RM 45,000 after some discounts.

Truly, God is so faithful, providing for the necessary funds, and even in excess.

Pastor Johnny's cup overflowed, as God poured down His blessings. He went home cured, with an overflowing blessing of RM20,000 extra, thanks to God's faithfulness.

What did I learn from this testimony?

Our Father is the richest Person on planet earth, and He supplies all our needs and our 'Cup overflows.'

In Luke 15:31, God says (and I receive): "All that I have is yours."

Testimony # 020   Retinal Detachment in Japan

I flew in to Japan on the first anniversary of the '9-11' terrorist attacks on the Twin Towers and the Pentagon.

The flight itself was surrounded by some domestic conflict, and I flew with a heavy heart. There were hardly any passengers on the flight, as everyone was afraid of a repetition of attacks during that first anniversary. I could stretch out on a five-row seating area and truly enjoyed the comfort and privacy of a nearly empty plane.

On arrival at Tokyo Narita airport, our group went on a roller-coaster bus trip till night fall, arriving in Nagano area late in the night. I was tired. The next day, the group visited Matsumoto castle and there was a lot of climbing and bending.

By evening, I felt a darkening of my vision on the right lower corner or quadrant. Just a few days before my flight to Japan, I had experienced some floatus in my eyes and was assured by my ophthalmology colleague after a brief assessment, that I was all right and that I could fly.

As soon as I reported my vision had been affected or that I was blind in my right lower quadrant, my colleague Dr Zak immediately brought me to see a senior fellow colleague who was a key office bearer for the conference.

A local Japanese doctor started to call around the area for an eye surgeon, but had difficulty finding one, as it was late Friday evening. Eventually, they managed to get a medical officer in Saku Hospital, and two of my local Japanese colleagues put me in a cab and off we went to Saku Hospital. I recall that it cost a hefty RM300 just to travel from the conference venue to the hospital.

On arrival, the kind medical officer of the eye unit checked me, and immediately confirmed that I had a retinal detachment. She showed me the picture of my retina confirming that there has been a retinal detachment in my right eye.

What should I do, now that I had fallen sick in a foreign land? This condition called a 'Retinal Detachment' was a serious one, requiring urgent surgery or one may go blind in that eye if the detachment extends. I worked it out, that without health insurance, the operation in Japan and stay for at least two weeks would cost me at least RM100,000. That would have been too much for me.

I prayed and pleaded with the LORD, "Please LORD, let me go home to Malaysia. LORD, you know that my left hand does not know what my right hand gives. Also, please do not let me be 'robbed' of RM100,000".

Meanwhile, I called Malaysia for advice from my good friend and experienced retinal surgeon Dr Lim. In Japan, Dr Zak had been my savior and Professor Tan had been so very helpful.

The local eye surgeon came to see me in the morning. I immediately asked him two questions, as suggested by Dr Lim.

The first being "Sensei, are you a retinal surgeon?", to which he replied, "No."

The second was: "Can I travel home safely to Kuala Lumpur?", to which he amazingly said, "Okay. But you must lie down horizontally all the time!"

My journey had begun, and clearly, it had to be the LORD's angels (dedicated to me), who was at hand to help me travel alone. For six legs of the journey, I successfully complied by being horizontal all the way, except for brief moments. From Hospital Saku to my hotel in Nagano, from the hotel to the train station at Nagano, on the train to Tokyo, from Tokyo train station to Tokyo Narita airport, on the flight from Japan to Kuala Lumpur KLIA Airport, and from KLIA Airport to Tung Shin Hospital, I travelled literally alone horizontally. Different individuals helped me along the way. At each juncture, I apologized to fellow travelers that I had to lie down horizontally.

God is truly faithful in bringing me out of Japan, being alone except for the first three legs, where a medical representative had accompanied me. I had travelled with help all along the journey, and in Tokyo train station, the Japanese assistant told me that this special route was used only by the Emperor when he travels. What a privilege.

I was operated successfully the next day by Dr Lim and my vision remains perfect at 20-20 (6-6) for the left affected eye. The total cost of surgery and stay was RM 4,000 or USD1,200 only. I experienced another miracle. Even though I was away from work for two weeks, it did not affect my income at all. I have no idea at all how there was no loss of income, despite me not working for half a month.

God had answered my prayer. He brought me home safely, and I was not 'robbed' of my precious financial resources. Staying in Japan for surgery would have cost me at least RM100,000 and a great deal of inconvenience to my family.

Before I left for Japan, at Nagano, Professor Tan prayed for me. Even in Tung Shin, at the early morning the next day, before going for the operation, I asked the LORD to send someone to pray for me, and Dr Michael appeared suddenly and committed the whole surgery to the LORD.

God had not only given me a divine blessing, but a royal one. His faithfulness and steadfast love is amazing. There were several miracles and answered prayers, following one mishap, - finding an eye doctor on Friday night, the green light to fly back, traveling back alone horizontally, angels sent to pray for me, cost of operation only RM4,000, no loss of income despite two weeks off, and full recovery of vision, eight in all. God is good and faithful. [Psalm 125:3, Hebrews 13:5]

What did I learn from this testimony?

Sometimes, in trials instead of looking at the mishap, consider the miracles and blessings as these trials allow God to show that He is forever faithful, and will never leave you nor forsake you. He is a miracle performing God, and we 'take for granted' the work of His angels by our side.

As He brought the Israelis out of Egypt, He brought me out of Japan, and performed eight miracles along the way, two less than for the Israelis.

Testimony # 021   God is my Healer

God is my Healer, and yours too. He has given us an amazing body that regenerates and repairs itself, apart from its ability to heal when wounded or damaged.

God has also given mankind wisdom to understand the human body, and go on further to develop the science of medical care.

However, there is the Divine Hand of God that heals either instantly or that begins a process of healing and recovery. I will describe two that I experienced.

Reverend Raymond Mooi, the Founder of the School of Acts came to preach one Sunday at my church (SIBKL in Kuala Lumpur), about 15 years ago. He was relating about the mission field and the various miracles that were taking place, and the signs and wonders that followed.

He said that there was a Cambodian lady who was blind and after prayer was able to see. Most of us, whenever we hear of such a testimony, we question the truth and reality of it, with a doubting approach; "Really?!"

It means that we doubt or do not believe immediately believe. Many hearts have been hardened so much that if we say we pray and even if the dead rose up to life, they would question and doubt. The common and frequent reply would be, "Really?", which means they will not 'really' believe.

I prepared my heart on that day and as soon as I heard the testimony by Reverend Mooi, I said within me, "Praise the LORD! hallelujah! I believe. I believe. Help my unbelief, LORD."

The message ended and an altar call followed. I stood up immediately among the congregation, and was awaiting a call for healing of the eyes, as I had just been operated for my eye and was in the recovery phase.

Pastor Raymond said nothing about the eyes, but instead mentioned bones and joints. I then realized that indeed, I had an issue with my right knee. Many years ago, when I was about fifteen, I had fallen from my bicycle and injured my right knee and developed what we call a hemarthrosis or blood in the knee joints. My parents had brought me to see a Chinese traditional doctor, who wrapped it in a poultice, leaving the swollen knee weeks to heal by itself.

Since then, the knee had never fully recovered and I even had a knee tapping once. Thus, for about six years prior, I could never do a full squat as my right knee was tight and had fluid inside all the time.

Pastor Raymond asked each of us to place our right hand over the injured bone or joint and I did so to my right knee.

In that instance, I was healed of an injured knee. I could squat down and sit on my heels like a Japanese lady. I went up on stage to testify that my knee was healed, doing a Japanese posture, and sitting on my heels.

Guess what, one doubter came up and asked me softly, "Really? You could not do that before."

I said, "Yes, this is the first time in six years that I have been able to bend my knees fully and squat. You can ask my son." He looked at my teenage son, who nodded in agreement.

It is strange that a believer can have so much unbelief. It is so important not to doubt because unbelief like faith can also grow into a boulder if not a mountain of doubt.

In another instance, some years after my retinal surgery, I felt a small area of poor vision over the same right quadrant. I was functionally all right, but occasionally would kick the foot of a table or chair. At a Bill Johnson and Randy Clark healing and miracle service in Thailand, Pastor Randy call out for miracles. I waited for the illness to be called out, and suddenly I heard one leader, Randy's assistant mention "Retinal Detachment", and I claimed it at once. Waving both hands over each lower quadrant, I begin to see both corners over the lower right and left, that meant I was being healed of that small corner on the right that had not yet fully received full vision.

"Hallelujah! I was healed!" This being the second time for the same eye, like the finishing touch that has given me full functional recovery in all my eye quadrants, each quadrant being a quarter of the visual field.

I am deeply grateful to the LORD for his healing hands. I can still do a Japanese sit down on my heels, some fifteen years after that healing, and it is now seventeen years since my retinal detachment and my vision is full and 6/6 on both eyes.

What did I learn from this testimony?

God is our Healer. All we need to do is believe and ask. Yes, there are anointed servants of the LORD whose prayers work miracles. Do not let unbelief quench the miracles in your life.

On your own, in your quiet little corner, between you and Jesus, seek your own divine healing.

Testimony # 022   Two Panic Attacks

Out there in the world, there are many, many people who suffer from various kinds of emotional, psychological and mental problems, including Christians. Even men and women of God can feel various kinds of issues of the mind. Yet, there are clear promises in the Scriptures that assure us that God has given us a sound mind, and that we can renew our minds, and most precious of all, that we have the mind of Christ Jesus.

One of the recently commonly diagnosed psychological disorders is called the "Panic Attack." God gave me the opportunity to experience two separate incidents where I suffered sudden "Panic Attacks", and He was there to intervene.

The first was when I was due to appear live on a morning television program called "Nona" where I was going to talk about "Migraine" to a live audience, and also take calls from the viewers.

Here was I at the adjourning room, all ready with makeup and touchup done, and about to enter the stage right in front of the camera. A local comedian was on 'live' and he had just finished his segment and I was next. This was not the first time I had been on live television, and I was already then, a mature, calm and steady experienced specialist and used to public speaking.

It was my turn in about one minute. Suddenly, fear and panic engulfed me, and I wanted to run out, and something in me had said, "No way am I entering! I cannot go on live television, in this state of mine!"

I was suddenly suffering from an acute panic attack. I had to fall back on my total trust in Jesus, and said this prayer, "Lord Jesus, help me. Take me through this live presentation. Calm me down, Lord."

I took a deep breath, and as soon as Imuda, the comedian came out, I was ready to enter.

As I entered, my heart was still beating fast, "Boom, boom, boom." I forced a smile, as I went in and sat down. The whole segment was lasted about 20 minutes, with my heart pounding away for most of it. My daughter had recorded the show for me. She did not see any signs of anxiety in me, and was also not aware of what I was going through, as she viewed the show live.

Time flies when you are "on air". It was over in a jiffy. I walked out, with face beaming, and heart still palpitating away, and gave thanks to my Lord for answering my prayers.

That night, when I got back, and viewed the live performance, I saw that I was as calm as any star performer. The presentation had been smooth and fluent, as if I was a real professional.

I gave thanks to God for His goodness.

Panic Attack No 2 took place right in the middle of a lecture, without a warning. Out of the blue, suddenly my mouth, lips and tongue began to freeze, and I felt I could not go on. There were about 200 medical and paramedical staff in the audience, and here was I stung and stunned for a couple of seconds.

I truly wanted to run out of the hall, and it was in the hospital where I was working in, and the audience knew me, and would probably have understood and accepted it if I quit midway.

I rejected the idea of stopping, and ignored that 'panic attack'. Instead, I put my total trust in my Lord Jesus, and just prayed silently a two or three worded prayer, "Lord, please help."

This time around, there was no palpitations, only dry lips, stiff tongue and rigid body. With that pause and prayer, I continued the lecture, though with a bit slower and more controlled delivery till the talk ended.

Phew! I was relieved when the lecture ended, and I forced a smile and left the lecture hall quietly. I never received a feedback, which meant that there were no obvious mistakes or noticeable 'anxiety' in me, like the previous live television presentation. Even though it may not have been the best lecture that I have given, I had sailed through the storm.

Again, I thanked God for His help and for answering my desperate prayers.

I went back to reflect on what had happened in those two instances of panic attacks, and came to the following conclusions. No matter, how good or fantastic or capable anyone is, we are mere mortals. We need to look after our physical, mental and emotional health.

On those two occasions, I had stretched myself physically, mentally and emotionally. I was tired on both occasions, with lack of sleep, and I was busy, very busy with a lot of things on my mind and I was troubled and disturbed over other things.

In that state of mind, body and emotions, I had become vulnerable, and was literally functioning on extra time, and stretched to the limits of my energy, which is not a healthy thing to do. That combination of a busy preoccupied mind, exhausted and not rested body, and disturbed emotions allowed 'the panic attacks' to be triggered. Medically speaking, when the blood sugar is low, and adrenaline is running high, together with other chemicals and minerals a little off the normal range, it was the right chemistry for disaster. Also, given the opportunity, I have no doubt that the unseen adversary would have capitalized on it, and contributed to further negative thoughts of failure, hopeless, fear and other symptoms. Fortunately, God intervened in my desperate prayer

Ever since then, I have been careful not to allow such a situation to occur and have never had another such episodes, though it is perfectly normal even for seasoned celebrities and sportsmen or women to experience a certain level of 'tension' just before the start of the event.

As a result of my two experiences, I have been able to assist a few patients who came to consult me about their panic attacks. I was able to intervene and assist them understand these attacks, without having to take medications and continue to feel handicapped and fearful.

I was able to convert so-called 'butterflies in the stomach' and "stage fright", as well as unexplained sudden panic into a peace and calmness, when I called upon the LORD.

God is our Healer and He can intervene in emergencies. Nevertheless, we have a responsibility to look after ourselves, our mind, body and emotions, for we literally and physically house the "temple of the Holy Spirit".

What have I learned from this testimony?

I am reminded that I am a mere mortal, and hence we should not stretch ourselves to the limits. Our body sends signals, most of which we should heed. When exhausted, we should rest; when sleepy, we should sleep; when hungry, we should eat; when thirsty, we should drink fluids. It is only during times of fasting, abstinence that we overrule these signals as training and preparation for the body, mind and soul.

Nevertheless, when in a state of panic or anxiety, or fear or danger, call upon The Lord for help and instant calm and peace will prevail, for He is the Prince of Peace.

Testimony # 023   My One-Stent Story

This is yet another story of God's healing Hand.

Three doctors died from sudden heart attacks during a certain season. I was directly involved in trying to resuscitate one of them. It was then that I decided that I needed to check my heart too. I did a heart scan and it showed some calcium in my arteries and the recommendations was to proceed with a full study called an angiogram.

The week before, there was an American man who was reported to have a 90% block on the screening scan. He allowed me to pray for him before the procedure. The angiogram was performed a week before mine, and "Lo, and behold, it was clear! There was no blockage!"

We both gave thanks to Jesus for answering our prayers.

My turn was next, the following week. I was very confident, since the week before this servant-son of the Most High had prayed and God had answered our prayers.

I was lying on the cardiac table, and the angiogram was going on, and not much was being said by my doctor-cardiologist-friend Dr Zain. Normally, a fellow colleague would shout out the good news and say, "It's all fine." Thus, his silence was ominous.

Dr Zain said, "Sng, one of your major arteries is 40-50% blocked. We will have to stent it." My wife was in the waiting area, and they were about to discuss the next step, which included an IVUS (or study of the artery from inside the artery).

My instant response was: "What happened, LORD?" - asking with all humility and reverence. I was surprised, but definitely not angry, bitter or frustrated, but truly seeking an explanation from the LORD.

This is one of the few instances in my life that an audible answer from the LORD came immediately.

He spoke gently and clearly, and I repeat the words verbatim: "My son, I gave your mother a perfectly healthy baby 58 years ago."

[My dear reader, both believer and non-Christian, I stand on oath that, it was exactly what I heard.]

Almost at once, I understood and interpreted it correctly. God had given a healthy baby to my parents 58 years before, and over the years, like a new BMW, there are issues and problems related to wear and tear. It is not the manufacturer's fault. The word that came strongly out to me was 'maintenance'. I had not been taking care of my health.

Over the past decade prior, as a busy doctor in private practice, my lunch was often delayed and it ended up being substituted by a packet of groundnuts and a few butter buns.

All these reflections took place over a couple of minutes.

As soon as I heard the first answer, I shot my next question, which came from my heart.

"But LORD, last week, I prayed for some one and he was healed completely. I feel discouraged now." I was referring to the American man.

Again, I heard the reply which came within seconds: "Son, when you pray, I use you as a vessel for My Glory."

I understood it at once and was at peace. I said, "Thank you, LORD."

The case was settled. One stent was inserted. Since then, I am very much more careful what I eat, and has been in relatively good health for a decade since.

What have I learned from this testimony?

We are mere mortals, and we can fall sick. It is our responsibility to take care of our body, mind and spirit. God is our Healer always, and He will restore us to good health, when we seek of Him.

Testimony # 024   Weak Vocal Cords

I thank God for good health generally. Apart from the knee, one-stent, I have good health, all my years.

However, due to weak vocal cords, I suffer from laryngitis quite often and have actually lost my voice a total of eight times. These are times when my voice comes down to zero or near zero. At the time of this writing, I am experiencing my 8th voice loss!

For every episode, I have recovered well, fully and even with a stronger voice, as I pray each time for new and renewed vocal cords.

I recall one situation when I was due to speak in a camp and give a few messages that I was struck with laryngitis and the voice was down to 30-40%. I was not sure whether I could go through giving a few messages.

I prayed and the committee prayed and, "Praise the LORD", the messages were delivered with a stable voice, and at the end of the camp, my voice was still there and stable.

This short testimony is to give thanks and praise to a God who is always by my side, and always able to intervene when we need Him.

I also claim Exodus 23:25 that there will be "no sickness in my midst".

Exodus 23:25 "So you shall serve the LORD your God; And He will bless your bread and your water, and I will take sickness away from the midst of you."

I pray the prayer that John prayed for Gaius in 3 John 1,2, that "Beloved, I prat that you may prosper in all that you do, and be in health, just as your soul prospers."

What have I learned from this testimony?

It is so important to be healthy, so that we can do God's work and also when we are well, we too need to give thanks for He is our Healer, all the time.
The key is to serve the LORD our God, and He will keep us in good health.

Testimony # 025   Missing Passport

I was scheduled to fly to Surabaya, Indonesia for a mission trip, to speak to a group of new freshie University students. I had invited my father-in-law to come along with me.

As usual, about two days before the intended journey, I checked my bedroom drawer where I normally keep my passport, and could not find it. It was a season when I was travelling a bit more than usual.

My thoughts were: "Okay, it must be in my office." So, the next day, after work, I rummaged through my office drawer, and to my surprise, I could not find the passport.

"Hmm, how come? It must be at home." I was travelling the next day, and not knowing where your passport is does make me somewhat anxious.

On arrival back home, I did a more thorough search and to my disappointment, I could not find it.

"It has to be in the office," I thought, after my third detailed failed search.

My flight was late in the afternoon, and I had to pick my father-in-law at around noon. As usual, I would still enter my office, clear up some work, before flying off.

I then decided to get in early to search for my passport. I got in at around 8 a.m. and did my search, and could not find my passport, after an hour! This was really serious and desperate. I had to fly as the meeting was scheduled that night, with me as a main speaker. It would take a couple of days to prepare a new passport then. Even if we rushed it, it would take a few hours, and that was just not possible.

I was really desperate! I literally sat down on the floor of my office, and cried in my heart, "Help me, Lord Jesus."

Suddenly, like a "bingo!", a thought came into my mind, that it was in the house, in an unlikely place, where I have never kept my documents, except for this particular time.

The Holy Spirit literally recalled to me that time when I rushed back and, in a hurry, just dropped my passport in the drawer of my home 'office', used more by my wife rather than me.

I immediately called home, as my daughter was still around. She did not pick up the phone, and we did not have a land line by then. I called a few times, but the phone was switched off.

Of course, I could have driven home and back, a trip that was about an hour. I had promised to pick up my father-in-law by ten, and it was 9 a.m.

A God or Holy Spirit prompting dropped into my mind. Call the neighbor! It is so important to have friendly neighbors, when one is in need.

She picked up the phone. Great!

"Please LC, I desperately need to contact Grace as I think my passport is downstairs. Will you please go over and call her? Her phone is switched off."

LC went and unfortunately my doorbell was not working. She knocked on the door and there was no response, as Grace is a fairly deep sleeper.

"I am sorry Doc but Grace is not answering."

A second Godly idea came. It was not very nice, but I was desperate.

"I am sorry, but please use the hose to shoot water on her window pane. I am sorry."

I could hear her say softly, "oh dear!", with an embarrassed laugh. LC did it, and Grace woke up came down to the door! She checked the office drawers and found my passport there and send it to me just in time.

I arrived in Malang, Surabaya in time with my father-in-law and we had an awesome meeting that night.

As a keen traveler and video photographer, he was ready with his gadget and recorded parts of the event. It was probably mind blowing for him to see nearly a thousand young Polynesian youths from the Indonesian archipelago jumping up and down praising the LORD.

This sight is out of the world for many Malaysians who have not been to an Indonesian church.

What did I learn from this testimony?

The LORD is my bailor and helper. He gets us out of trouble, even when it is wholly our fault, and our mistakes. We can still depend on Him, as recorded in Psalm 118:8 emphasizing that we can trust in the LORD always. He indeed is my help in times of desperation. More of such testimonies to follow.

Testimony # 026   The Lost Button

It is probably no big deal, one may say. A small matter indeed, but my LORD is always there to give me a hand, to help me and to solve my problems. He has a massive network and team of angels at His dispatch and command, and they obey Him instantly.

I was walking in the streets of London, some three decades ago, when suddenly I found one button missing from my shirt. It was a light blue button, matching my white shirt with striking blue vertical stripes. One thing I felt sure was that it was not easy to find the same button to match the others. Besides, this was a busy street in London, not my bedroom or in my office, where I can literally sweep the floor or comb every corner for a little button.

I was a young Christian then, still on my honeymoon with the LORD and on fire, and full of faith. I knew that the LORD will find the button for me, and of course, He knows where it had dropped. He knows everything.

I said a little prayer, and then began my search. I did not stoop down or crawl but just walked casually, on that cool autumn day, while the sun was still up and providing good natural light.

Within 5-10 minutes, I saw the button or to make it more interesting, the button saw me! I gave thanks to God for His faithfulness. God is my perfect finder. Before Google search, there was God. Would I find my button if I typed "Find button in London", or tell my phone, "Google, where is my button?"

With my LORD, I could. He found the button for me.

What have we learned from this testimony?

There is nothing too small or too big to ask from our Father. He is so very obliging, so ever willing to help, and it does not matter what time of the day it is, He will be there to help. Only ask Him, then seek in the area of concern, and `knock' go right down to the ground and put in the effort. And, of course, you must believe.

Testimony # 027   Missing Document Found at Eleventh Hour

There are probably many ways to describe people. If the level of being organized is one of the ways, I would fall nearer the lower range of being disorganized. On a scale of 0-10, I am not fastidious as to where I put my things, how I file my things, and I lack a proper system, even until now. Hence, I would not rate myself more than a '3'. One may love to hire a personal secretary with an ability of 8-9 score, but not want to live with someone with an obsessive `10'. A couple with a score of 1-2 each would be a disaster, perhaps. Here is the testimony.

I have great difficulty keeping my documents in the right place, and filing them up in the right file, except for 'my passport'! Thus, at that time, when I had a private limited company (plc) or Sendirian Berhad, in our Malaysian language, we needed bank documents to be sent in on time for auditing.

I found this exercise a painful chore every year. I recall one particular year, when I was stretched to the last hour, the last day in fact, where I had to send in my document by the next day. The dateline had arrived. Everything was in order, except for one single page of a certain month.

I just somehow could not find that particular document, a mere sheet of document, yet vital as a last piece in a jigsaw puzzle. I searched and searched and searched but to no avail. It just could not be found. And I needed it by the next day, and it was already behind schedule, and a late submission could mean a fine.

In desperation, I sat down on my first-floor family room area, next to where my cabinet was kept, and literally `cried' to the LORD from my heart. This form of 'cry' is different from the weeping of sorrow, or the weeping in true repentance, but a groaning desire for help from within the depths of my soul, my inner being. [Romans 8:23]

"Help me please, Lord Jesus. Help me find my document, please."

After about ten minutes, I stood up, and gently opened my steel cabinet, which was full of my office files and documents. I just placed my hand randomly into one of the slots, and my hand felt a single document and I pulled it out.

Would you believe it? I was stunned with shock to see that it was the 'missing document'.

It just has to be the Hand of God, working through His Holy Spirit and angels that helped me find the single missing document.

That missing document was found in the eleventh hour, thanks to God through His Helping Hand, after a desperate prayer.

What have I learned from this testimony?

We have an awesome God, and if we walk with Him, and He is always by our side, as a Friend, Helper, Teacher, Guide, Counsellor, Protector, Healer, Master and our God.

He hears our prayers. In sheer desperation, just 'groan' and 'grind' in your prayer closet, and He will reply and act.

Testimony # 028   Tsunami Story – Calling Upon the Christian God

This is an amazing testimony related to me by two different persons from two different regions affected by the devastating tsunami of December 2004.

I am sure that there are many amazing and awesome stories of the tsunami, but this one, from the salvation point of view must surely stand out as one of the most, if not the most significant one.

It is my practice to greet my patients from abroad with a very warm welcome followed by questions about their nation and community. I receive a fair number of patients from Indonesia and a good number come from Acheh.

It breaks my heart when I hear of some of their stories. One particular Indonesian male patient told me when I enquired, that he had lost over 300 relatives, literally all of his relatives. The moment he felt some tremors, he had packed his family into their van and driven off in a hurry. When he returned, he saw the massive devastation that had wiped out his whole village and all his 300 relatives.

This testimony however is not about him, but about a middle-aged Muslim Indonesian lady who had come for a medical checkup. I did not enquire about her loss of relatives, but asked gently about how the shocking experience. In all my enquiries, the questions come with a wave of compassion for the community, not from curiosity.

She voluntarily told me this in the Indonesian language, which is very similar to my own national language, or Malay language, and I shall write down the exact words she said, both in the native language as well as the translated English words.

She said, "Doctor, during the peak of the tsunami, I heard the people cry."

"What did they say?" I asked, as I shared her grief and sorrow, though it was probably over five years after the great tsunami of December 2004, at the time of our conversation.

They cried out, "God of the Christians, help us; God of the Christians, help us."

[Tuhan orang Kristian, tolong kami; Tuhan orang Kristian, tolong kami.]

I was a little surprised hearing this from a Muslim Indonesian lady, but did not think very much of it, nor did I comment further, as I went on to complete my medical examination.

A few weeks later, a Pastor friend of mine told me that he and wife had met a Malaysian lady in Kuala Muda, Kedah who told her that during the tsunami, she had heard the people cry out loud. When questioned further as to what did they said, she replied:

"Tuhan orang Kristian, tolong kami; Tuhan orang Kristian, tolong kami."

Translated into English, it meant, "God of the Christians, help us; God of the Christians, help us."

Almost at once, when I heard the second testimony, I received the interpretation below. It was so strong a revelation, that I believe it is the Holy Spirit's prompting and revelation to me.

The first insight that I received from the Holy Spirit is that during a thunderstorm, heavy rain or any small or big flood, certainly in the great tsunami of 2004, it is impossible to hear the voices or cries of any human being, within even fifteen feet from where one is.

In other words, the two ladies certainly could not and did not hear anyone nearby crying. I tested this hypothesis, and found that if anyone is in the shower, he or she cannot hear even if you shout or call out to that person when you are several feet away, or at least cannot the words spoken would not be audible or understood. Likewise, in a heavy thunder storm, you will not be able to hear anyone across the road talking. Furthermore, if you really did hear any cries, you would be in the same waters drowning too.

So, what did they hear? The revelation that I received from the Holy Spirit is this.

In any desperate situation, anyone will cry out for help, and each one would cry out to their God, gods or whoever they are worshipping. Remember the story of Jonah, when the sailormen all cried and prayed to their respective gods, as they knew that they were close to perishing.

Thus, as these thousands upon thousands were drowning in the waters, their cries rose up from the Indian Ocean in those few seconds, and they did reach the ears of the Almighty for sure, as this is a very large number of voices simultaneously crying out to the heavens.

In His Mercy and Compassion, since our LORD is a very merciful and compassionate God, THE LORD GOD gave a last chance for everyone perishing and told them to call out to Him.

This is the exact script or words that I received, and I believe, as the Holy Spirit prompted me with this revelation that THE LORD spoke from Heaven with a clear and loud booming voice that everyone drowning heard and received:

"I am the God of the Christians, call Me."

When one hears a voice from Heaven, its sound, its clarity, its loudness and its piercing of the heart, one knows that it is an authentic voice from Heaven.

I believe that almost everyone responded in desperation and called out to the LORD, and said:

"God of the Christians, help us; God of the Christians, help us."

These voices almost in unison rose up from the Indian Ocean, travelled upwards and throughout the region and its echoes were supernaturally heard by two different Muslim ladies in two different regions of two different countries, but were related directly to this author, or indirectly through another party.

On a recent visit to Batam, just a week before this final draft was being submitted to the press, one brother confirmed that this was what a lot of people heard, as this news was televised on national television over three days, following the tsunami.

The Bible says in Romans, "He who calls upon the Name of the LORD will be saved."
Joel 2:32, Acts 2:21 and again in Romans 10:13

I believe we will meet many hundreds of thousands of tsunami victims who perished but made it into Heaven, when they called out to the God of the Christians.

What an amazing and awesome testimony of God's compassion, mercy and faithfulness to His Word and His Name, which is above all names.

What did I learn from this testimony?

How in desperate trouble, call upon the Name of the LORD. He hears, He sees, He knows and He cares, and He will help.

Testimony # 029   Another Tsunami Story – Nearly washed away

This is my second tsunami story as related by my church elder SK Ng. He has kindly given me permission to relate his story. He was with his family of four in Phuket by the beach, at the time of the tsunami.

It was their last day in Phuket, and their original plan was to enjoy the beach for their last morning. Somehow, at about 4.30 a.m. in the morning, SK's wife, whom we call sister Hui woke up with a decision that they should gather at 10.00 a.m. that morning in their hotel room to wait upon the LORD to plan for the next year 2005. They were staying on the 7th floor of the hotel by the beach.

So, on the morning of that fateful day of December 26th, each woke up with their own itinerary but with the agreement to meet up at 10.00 a.m. in the room.

SK decided to return the car they had rented, so he drove down to the town. One daughter decided to enjoy the beach, going for a walk, and she visited the washroom, which was at ground level by the pool.

Dutifully, they arrived back on time in their rooms just before 10.00 a.m.

According to reports, the deadliest tsunami in history started at 7.59 a.m. in the Indian Ocean off Sumatra, hitting Acheh in 20 minutes, and arriving in Thailand between 1 ½ to 2 hours, which meant that SK's two children had just missed the first wave within minutes.

With the first wave, the commotion was enough for SK and family to look down and they saw some rubble. They called the reception and were informed by the desk that it was advisable to move to higher ground, and some residents did so. Imagine the risk for those who moved upwards but were not in time as the second wave came quite soon after.

SK and family decided to stay put as they were on the 7th floor. In the meantime, they had tuned on the television and discovered soon after that there had been an earthquake and a big tsunami affecting the region. In the news, it was mentioned that 16 people had died in the tsunami. By the time the second wave struck, SK and family knew that it was a devastating tsunami. He tried to make contact for his travel to the airport as his flight was at 7.30 p.m. local time, but without success, as most lines were down. Finally, he managed to get a friend from Bangkok to make arrangements, and they were transported successfully to the airport.

It was a great relief to be on the plane, as the air of death and disaster was in the air by then. Strangely too, but not unexpectedly, the plane was nearly empty.

It was on their return to Kuala Lumpur, when the news had spread all over the world that SK and family realized that they were just minutes from death, if not for Hui's decision to call a family meeting at about the same time the tsunami hit Phuket.

Clearly, it was God's divine protection on this family, who has been faithfully serving the LORD as my church's elder for many years. In fact, that daughter who was saved from drowning is now happily married to the son of my church's senior Pastor.

What did I learn from this testimony?

When we are walking with the LORD, and a disaster of whatever magnitude or scale is near or looming, God will save us from that situation. In short, when the time is not due, we will not perish.

Testimony # 030   God's Protection on Malaysia from Tsunami

Can a country be 'saved' or 'spared' of a disaster that badly affected it neighbors? The great devastating tsunami of December 2004 took a total of 230,000 lives, with Indonesia suffering

130,000 deaths, Sri Lanka 31,000, Indian 10,700, Thailand 8,200, Myanmar 600 and even distant Somalia 212 victims. Malaysia, shielded by the northern tip of Sumatra had 73 deaths, far less than tourists from eight other countries.

We count it a great blessing that our northern region was so near, but spared because of Sumatra.

This is what my family and I experienced while we were on holiday in the northern part of Pangkor Island, receiving just a late flash of low gushing water from the Indian Ocean and Andaman Sea.

It may not have been so dramatic as in the previous two stories but it was close.

My family was holidaying in Pangkor Island, which is situated in the Straits of Malacca. There were four of us, as our daughter was in the United Kingdom then.

We had a relatively quiet Christmas night, as there was no Christmas party. However, me and my two sons decided that we should sing carols and the local band at hand was kind and obliging, and the leader of the band was a Christian, named Paul.

We sang a few carols and there were perhaps less than a dozen of us around for the countdown. Yet, we decided a countdown was good thing to do.

We started from 10, 9, 8 and down and when we reach zero, we had a sudden downpour on the dot as heavy rain hit the roofs. All of us present were startled and did not know what to make out of it.

With that we went to bed. In the morning, at around 8 a.m. I was looking out from the room towards the beach, and feeling the peace, even though it was exactly towards the direction of the tsunami, because the cove and beach faced the north.

Some villagers told us, at around 9 a.m. that an earthquake had hit the Sumatra and some of them had felt the tremor. We felt nothing.

We checked out, and headed for the pier, as the boat was scheduled to pick us up at 2 p.m. While waiting there, we and the people around us saw a fast current going past us. The local folk commented that it was very odd to see the water flow at such speed, like in a river, he had commented.

The boat that was meant to pick us up struggled to dock and took about 15 minutes. It got some of us irritated when we did not understand what was happening.

We were actually experiencing the late gush of water from the Andaman Sea as a result of the tsunami, coming in two or three waves, though by then the level of the water was low, but the speed was fast.

We crossed over to the mainland, picked up our car and drove off happily. It was around 3.30 p.m. by then, that our daughter called to check on us.

She told us that a massive tsunami had struck Sumatra, and asked how we were.

On record, we found out later that parts of Penang, Langkawi and Kedah were affected badly by the tsunami with a total of 73 lives were lost. That number is very small compared to the 230,000 who perished.

If we look at the map of Sumatra, and the epicenter of the earthquake, we must thank God that Malaysia was protected by the northern tip of Sumatra, and had the tsunami hit the Indian Ocean a little higher, the whole of the northern region of West Malaysia especially Penang would have had massive casualties, and even Pangkor where I was would have been badly hit, and me and my family were right there on the pier when the fast but shallow waters passed by.

Malaysia was saved by a whisker! My family too. We thank God for His divine protection of my family and my nation.
As a late effect of the distant tremor, my back kitchen on the fifth day of the tsunami suddenly gave a loud sound and over 100 small tiles were lifted up, in a few seconds.

After the tsunami, there were two kinds of sermons, one that related it was God who was punishing the people, and the other who related that the enemy was the destroyer. I will not enter this debate, but what is clear is this: that the slightest shift of things i.e. the geography of the earth can cause massive devastation, and it is God who sustains planet earth. He is sovereign and is always in control.

What did I learn from this testimony?

There are many ifs here; if we were in Phuket instead, or if we were in Langkawi or Penang, or if the epicenter was a little further north. One thing for sure, even with the massive devastation, God was in control on the destiny of every city, every village, every life. We must believe that.

My country and my people were saved from a major disaster. I believe it was God's protection on Malaysia.

Testimony # 031   100-Fold Multiplication

I was travelling down to the city center to attend postgraduate lectures in London, when I met my fellow church member.

"Hi Kim, join me for one of the special Morris Cerullo meeting at Kensington Temple. You will be blessed." Kim was my middle name then, which I used for convenience as it was difficult to pronounce or remember my surname.

I felt prompted to go along, skipping classes for that day. Coincidentally, I had just withdrawn 50 sterling pounds from the nearby teller.

Brother John from the ministry was speaking; he was very persuasive as he spoke and ministered on giving, and giving generously. He declared that God will bless the cheerful giver, and can even multiply our generosity over 100 times.

Hallelujah! I believed and prayed. When the altar call came, I gave cheerfully the 50 Sterling Pounds I had just withdrawn, and believed too that God will multiply my funds a hundred-fold in return. As a young Christian then, I was full of faith, and my heart was pure and sincere.

A few weeks after that love offering, I returned to my home country, to Sarawak, Borneo where I was posted then. I visited my bank and to my pleasant surprise, I found my account balance to be in excess of RM 15, 000, - a 100-fold blessings returned!

From my own estimation, after my regular withdrawal every month from the same account, at the most, there would only have been RM2, 000 in it. There was an excess of RM15, 000, which I could not explain until today.

God had indeed multiplied my offering a hundred times and deposited it into my accounts.

You may doubt and disbelieve, but I received it and took it a one-hundred-fold blessing from God. All glory and praise to my LORD for His goodness and faithfulness.

What did I learn from this testimony?

God is faithful in His Word and does miracles and wondrous things for his beloved. We can never out give God.

Testimony # 032   Give me Money LORD

Going into private practice was a major move for me. I had resisted it for a long time mainly because I was afraid that "money would corrupt me spiritually."

A man of God came from India. He was in great need. I believed in him. His testimony is true and his fruits were clear and evident, as his work has raised nearly 400 village churches over two decades of work when I first met him. I tried to raise funds for him, for as a government servant with a basic salary, I had little extra and hardly any savings. I contacted about ten millionaires to help, and came back with "zero" offerings.

In my frustration, I came before the LORD and declared, "I want money now. Give me money, so that I can bless the church."

With that in 1999, I started my private practice after miraculously obtaining my early retirement. I vowed to the LORD that I would give half my time to Him, if He would double my income.

That was an easy feat for Him, for in the very next month, my income doubled to twice my government salary.

Apart from blessing me with a good income, and "my cup overflows", He sends generous donations at times of needs and requests. One thing is my personal life, as far as finances are concerned is that "I do not hoard." I also do not know how to handle large sums of funds. Thus, if I should suddenly receive a billion ringgit, I would not know what to do with it, except to part with it, and give it away.

The key in riches comes in Luke 16:10-12, which relates that we must be trustworthy with the little money we are given, before God will release His Heavenly funds to us, funds which are legally ours, in the first place. To say that you will give when you become as rich as Bill Gates is an incorrect principle, if you understand these verses.

Luke 16:10-12, "He who is faithful in what is least is also faithful in much; he who is unjust in what is least is also unjust in what is much. Therefore, if you have been unfaithful in unrighteous mammon, who will commit to you trust, the true riches? And if you have not been faithful in whatever is another man's, who will give you what is your own?"

These are the words of Jesus. This means that if you have been given some money to use as yours, and you do not use it well, you are being tested. It is the faithfulness in your handling of the monies that will open the door for your own heavenly assigned riches to befall and bless your coffers. Try it.

This is a short testimony with one purpose, to remind us that the source of all riches is the LORD. Thus, I only began to ask ABBA Father for money in 1999, and I have been faithful as in Luke 16, and thus it releases the full wealth to us when we have been faithful to the end.

What have I learned since asking God for money?

All of us need money and funds, and ABBA Father gives freely when we ask. When we have been faithful to the little, He has provided, then He will shower His riches on us, because He promises in Luke 15:31 that "all that I have is yours.".

Testimony # 033 Giving 10% of my First Fruits

The word came to me as a reminder at least once from Proverbs 3:9-10.

It says: "Honor the LORD with your possessions, and with the first fruits of all your increase; So, your barns will be filled with plenty and your vats will overflow with new wine."

I did that after my request for money. Like Abraham, I gave ten percent of my first private practice earnings to a Bishop and prophet, who prayed and blessed me.

It has been two decades now since that first day.

Mid way through, I shifted after ten years to another hospital selling of the premise that I had purchased as my office. I made a profit of about RM 880, 000 on paper. The same word came to me as a reminder. I faithfully divided a tenth into ten portions of RM8, 888 each and blessed eight ministers of the LORD. My daughter Grace, who was in Bible school then received a double portion from me.

One minister told me that one of her students had come forward to give a word of prophecy that she would be receiving a windfall, and she did receive a cheque for RM8, 888. Another minister was also delighted that the funds had come in at that special time of need.

God wants us to be cheerful givers. I am so touched by how a little blessing opened the doors for others to move on, get on with their lives, and even go on to higher grounds.

The blessings that we have received are meant to be shared. The poor and the sick will always be around, perhaps as a mission field, both for us to exercise our compassion, as testing ground for the rest of us who always have enough.

It is far better to be a lender or giver than a borrower, and as one gives and gives and gives, we will break through the barrier of selfishness, hoarding, stinginess, and the love of money, almost like breaking the sound barrier.

My breakthrough came when I broke my barrier of six digits, related in another testimony.

Giving must come from the heart, and as one gives, the heart to give enlarges, and one experiences a special joy to help, give and donate.

It is true that you can take a billion dollars to a poor country in Africa, or in countries where there is a lot of poverty e.g. India, and it will vanish in a month. Giving is not blindly throwing cash in the streets for all. In those few crazy instances when cash is freely given in public, people have died from stampede and accidents.

The poor is beside you, around you and near you, and many knocks on your doors for help. You need not go out to seek them.

What have I learned from this testimony?

Giving does not hurt; giving till it hurts will in fact make you a cheerful giver.

Testimony # 034   Giving Until it Hurts

The breakthrough comes when we give until it hurts, and that breakthrough makes one a cheerful giver. This is a personal story about a man I know.

This is probably similar to training in sports where the athlete pushes himself or herself to the limits of his or her tolerance and then makes that breakthrough improvement, smashing world records. The same applies in bodybuilding where the muscle tears and then regenerates.

Giving is like that too. Christians are taught to tithe, and parting with that 10% is often painful to some people, and thus, many remain there at 10% and become what I refer to as the "stingy Christian."

When this man was saved, he gave his first tithe amounting to around RM200 [RM is Malaysian ringgit, where 1USD is equivalent to about 4RM]. That amount gradually increased to RM300, and then RM400 as his salary increased over the next few years. It can 'hurts' to give that amount away, as one often thinks that it could be used for personal needs. For the Bible to say that God loves a cheerful giver, it means that He knows that the rest of them give grudgingly or with some degree of sorrow!

Yet, God knows that too, and He is preparing the believer for the special breakthrough that we read in Luke 16:10-12. After all, Jesus promised that He came to give us life, and life in abundance.

Luke 16:10-12, "He who is faithful in what is least is also faithful in much; he who is unjust in what is least is also unjust in what is much. Therefore, if you have been unfaithful in unrighteous mammon, who will commit to you trust, the true riches? And if you have not been faithful in whatever is another man's, who will give you what is your own?"

The next breakthrough came for this person was when he went into business. His income jumped to five figures for the first time, thus stepping up the tithe to the tune of RM2,000 monthly.

The next jump came when there was a need for a building fund in a local Chinese Church connected to the church this person was serving in. He purchased a table for a significant amount and invited many wonderful widows along.

Then came the big breakthrough test, as the reader would have noticed the jump in multiples of ten from 200 to 2,000 to 20,000. That was exactly what happened when he reached the age of 55 and was able to withdraw my providence fund.

It was a significant sum of money that became available suddenly. The Spirit of God prompted this man to write out a single cheque for a significant sum, a leap of faith for a man of God, whose good work over three decades were evident.

This man suddenly broke through the 'pain barrier' and became a cheerful giver, even pledging to the Kingdom that the next offering would take another jump, and a final legacy to the Kingdom of God would be a further sum to be bequeath to the LORD's work.

It did not hurt any more, and this man had moved or transited into a new realm of generosity, happily sharing from the heart. His left hand does not know what the right hand does.

One thing is for sure, all that this man's Father in Heaven has now belongs to him, for He said, "All that I have is yours." Luke 15:31

In conclusion, we are all God's steward of whatever we hold on His behalf; we of course do need wisdom and graciousness to invest and share these riches, all for His Kingdom. By all means, bless yourself, your immediate family and your beloved ones, and allow others to share your blessings, for we are all co-inhabitants and co-heirs of this great Kingdom.

There are two truths here : one is that we will never be able to bring one cent across to Heaven and we do not need to, secondly, we are only stewards of our wealth and riches, because we are here on borrowed time, and all that we have actually belongs to God.

The poor is always around us; and it is always far better to give than to borrow; besides, when we give to the poor, we actually lend to God, and He does not remain a debtor to you for long, as He will repay.

Proverbs 19:17 "He who has pity on the poor lends to God; and He will pay back what he has given."

What have I learned from this testimony?

Giving and generosity is a process, and a journey best learned by each own in each one's own time and capacity. When we have been so richly blessed and have excess, we should share our blessings.

Testimony # 035   God Grants my Heart's desires

This testimony is about the truth in God's Word, as He gives us the desires of our heart.

Psalm 37:4. "Delight yourself also in the LORD, and He shall give you the desires of your heart."

In other words, whatever you want or wish, even before you pray, the LORD grants it to us, to those who walk with Him and delights in Him.

I will relate two things, one on food and the other on possessions.

Durian is to many Malaysians the 'king of the fruits.' Malaysians and many people from Asia love it, and the craze has now spread to China, which is a huge market for the best quality durians, called the "Musang King."

However, as a fruit it is difficult to obtain due to demand and popularity, and recently because of a very high commercial interest from abroad, namely China. Secondly, it is a heavy and prickly fruit and messy to buy, apart from the costs. Choosing a good durian from an honest durian seller can be a challenge. More often than not, the innocent customer is cheated and ends up paying for a poorer quality or lower grade fruit and at a higher price. Thirdly, when you have bought it, it is a task to open the fruit and get access to the lovely fleshy fruit. This does not include the fact that the fruit is not socially acceptable in public, and is banned in many premises especially hotels and on the airplane. One who consumes the fruit often carries the odor with it in your hands, or worse still when you let out a burp in public.

For those reasons, I hesitate to buy it myself, but being attracted to the smell, I often have that desire. More than once, just thinking about it, desiring it, and not willing to make the effort to buy it, I get surprised when a call comes through.

"Doc, we have some durians! Come and join us tonight."

Or, "Doc, drop by and pick up some durians. We have got them from our farm."

God truly knew my desire and grants it to me, when I was thinking about it. As far as the durian story goes, I have now dropped it from my wish-list and no longer desire to consume durians. This is a personal choice. I have joined the group of non-durian eaters, especially foreigners, who now cannot bear to come near the smell of durians.

The next testimony is about my love for pens. I love pens, especially expensive and beautiful fountain pens. I have Parker, Pilot, Sheafers, and even won a set of beautiful Elysee pens, sold through the local agent Staedtler.

In recent years, I began to have a desire and wish to own a Mont Blanc pen. I glanced through one advertisement that there was a special offer and off I went to purchase one at a cost of RM250 or USD 60 which is considered cheap and affordable, at that time.

I kept it with me for a few months and did not use it. One day, I felt the need to give an expensive gift to a dear friend, and I did just that – give my precious Mont Blanc pen. God however knew that I still wanted to own a Mont Blanc pen badly. That was my heart's desire, but I would not go out to buy one.

My sister came by from Australia and had bought my eldest brother one, but since he was busy and did not meet up, she passed it to me just before she flew off.

Yes, I now have a Mont Blanc pen, given to me finally.

I was preaching on Christmas Day in Chennai, and the title of my message was 'The PRESENT', with each letter referring to an aspect of a gift or present, being directly referring to God's precious gift to us in the form of a Savior.

The letter 'S' referred to the adjective 'Special' which means that a good present cannot be ordinary but should be of value. I then spontaneously turned to my wonderful and efficient interpreter Pastor Babu, who had been so good in interpreting my message from English to Tamil. I said that for the good work Pastor Babu was doing and had been doing the past few days, he deserved a good present, something truly of value, such as this, and I took out the Mont Blanc in my pocket and put it into his, and said to him, "This pen is now yours!"

After the message, I sat down and was now without my Mont Blanc pen. Within seconds of my sitting down, someone tapped my shoulder and said, "Doc, the Holy Spirit told me to give you this Mont Blanc pen," and he put his Mont Blanc pen into my left-hand pocket.

I gave thanks to God for that. I got a Mont Blanc pen back.

A few weeks or months later, back in Kuala Lumpur, I met up with my brother, who mentioned our sister in passing. I recalled about the pen and therefore passed the Mont Blanc pen that was in my pocket to him.

I was once again now without a Mont Blanc pen. It wasn't long before, a grateful patient, without my asking gave me a high-end gold-plated Mont Blanc pen. As my son was graduating in medicine at Cambridge University, I decided to give him that precious gold Mont Blanc pen as a recognition of his successful study and graduation from Emmanuel College of Cambridge.

I was now again without a Mont Blanc pen. That was the fourth precious pen given away by me. But the desire to own one was still very strong. On my 63rd birthday, I held a thanksgiving dinner, and guess what? One of the guests gave me a Mont Blanc pen, an appreciation for looking after her mother.

This Mont Blanc pen is still with me up until the present moment.

Guess what, my cup overflowed when during the last Christmas, a generous person gave me a set of two Mont Blanc pens, which means that I now have three Mont Blanc pens.

Recently, I gave another one away to my son and am now remain a proud owner of two Mont Blanc pens, one fountain and one ball point pen.

In total, I have received six Mont Blanc pens, bought one and given to me six, and I have given four away. God truly gives me the desires of my heart.

What have I learned from this testimony?

God's love for us is so special, and when we reciprocate and love Him and delight in Him, amazing things happen. One of them is the way He grants us the desires of our heart.

Testimony # 036   God Grants my Wish: "Two Months in Holland"

Desires are something that one longs for in our hearts. They may not be on our prayer list, and we may not voice it out to others or even pray about it. Yet, it is definitely something strong and passionate in our hearts.

I relate another random wish that I uttered in my mind and then forgot about it, until it came to pass. I was in Kuala Terengganu as a physician. It is a quiet town, and great place to have a family and to raise up kids. Yet, I somehow felt the tension, was so busy that on one of my little moments of stress, 'blurted' out in my hearts these thoughts.

"If only I could have just two months all by myself, away from all this busy work and from the family."

That is a strange and not so nice desire to have, but I did have that wish to be away from it all for a period of two months, to spend time with the LORD.

Many months passed after I had expressed that in my heart and forgotten, when I was offered a scholarship to have an internship in "Quality Assurance" in the Central Organization for Quality in Health in Holland, called CBO. At that time, Holland was among the recognized countries where quality assurance in Health Care was run at a national level and indicators of clinical care were being developed.

I was undecided whether to go or not. I had about a week to decide and thus, I told my family that I would pray about it. In the following week, there was a meeting or conference in Kuala Lumpur and I flew in from Kuala Terengganu. I had begun serious prayer, waiting upon the LORD to hear from Him, as to whether I should accept the scholarship offer and go to Holland for two months.

Guess what? On my second day of prayer and searching and asking, the answer came, while I was praying alone in the hotel I was staying in, in Kuala Lumpur.

I heard the Spirit of God say to me, "This offer to go abroad for two months is in answer to your prayer."

I was surprised with what I heard. I asked back, "What prayer?", as I had forgotten about that wish.

The Holy Spirit flashed back in my mind immediately the wish that I had blurted out in my heart – "to be away for two months."

That was my heart's desire. Hardly a prayer, just a mere wish or thought and God granted it, and reminded me that He had given me two months to be alone.

That really happened to me. I was in a quiet town of Utrecht. After work each day, I would be locked into my own room alone to read, read and read the Bible. My colleague on the same program must have wondered why I was such a quiet and uninteresting person, who would lock myself into the room, and hardly ever went out.

I had used all my time to read the Bible. In appreciation for the time that the LORD had given me, I decided to read through the Bible. I read voraciously and furiously, and in 6 weeks, consumed 65 books of the Bible, leaving Revelation for another season.

As the churches were in Dutch, I did not attend any church service in my two months there.

I received my wish – two months all alone by myself in a faraway land. And, of course, I did see some parts of Holland.

At the same time, the training that I received allowed me to further myself professionally and opened the door for my early retirement some years later.

What did I learn from this testimony?

When we really want something badly, passionately and really long for it like Hannah, God grants it to us, for we are His beloved.

Testimony # 037   Smashed Head During Sleep Walking

There is a myth that dreams and sleepwalking are harmless, and seldom pose a danger to the one who is dreaming.

My story and testimony are one such dreamer and dream that could have caused a lot of danger and harm.

It was during a season when I was on the antihypertensive medication called Betaloc or Metaprolol. This medication is known to increase dreams in those who take it. However, I am also a dreamer, in my spiritual walk, as I have had many, many Godly dreams, as I have related in some of my earlier testimonies.

In this particular dream, I was somehow at risk of being locked in an office, and I had to get out before the doors closed. Somehow, in rushing to get out, I tripped and fell. This far, whatever happened as described constitutes the dream.

It was around that time that my sleepwalking started, and the dream was still rolling on. Apparently, I had got up and stood upright on my bed, next to my wife who was on my left-hand side. Thank God also that the ceiling fan is relatively high and even while standing on the bed, with outstretched arms, it was safe as I am just under 5 ft 6 ins in height, being relatively short.

The door for exit in my dream was on my left. The master bedroom where my wife and I were sleeping in is on the second floor, and the windows were on the left side of the bed.

I headed for the exit in my dream while walking on the bed, and naturally tripped over my wife's legs and smashed my head directly on the wooden floor, from the height of the bed.

Thud! It hurt!! And I could hear the thud in my dream, but strangely while it hurt and I said, "Oh, my God,", I still did not wake up from my dream. In the dream, I was desperate to get out fast, as the door was going to close in on me any time, and it was only several feet away. I was also a few feet from the window that would have meant a fall from first floor if I exited from the window.

Because I fell, and it hurt, I prayed in my dream, as I often do. This was my prayer:

"Help me Father," as I laid down helplessly, both in dream and in the real situation at on the floor, by the bedside. My prayer was directed to God, to help me get up and get out in time. Meanwhile, as a result of the knock, I was dazed and could not proceed to get up and reach out for the door, which would have been my second-floor window. I may have actually had a brief moment of loss of consciousness.

As soon as I prayed, I heard a voice telling me to call upon Jesus. I immediately shouted out, "Jesus, Jesus!"

That woke my wife up and she called me and her calls to me woke me up from my dream!

I realized at once what had happened, and immediately called my daughter and asked her to send me to the emergency room for a head scan that night, as it was indeed a bad knock from a height of perhaps 7-8 feet.

Thank God as the scan was normal, and I decided to stay overnight in hospital. I did not suffer any residual symptoms from the concussion, and was back to work the next day.

What have I learned from this story?

This being one of the many times of my potential deaths or severe injury, we need to pray Psalm 91 over our lives regularly, and to commit our lives and our work to the LORD and He will bless and protect us.

I thank God for a shield of protection on my life, so that my stay on earth will continue until the its time to go home to my Father. My motto is clear: "To live is (for) Christ, to die gain."

Testimony # 038   Sharp Rebuke from God

Hearing God's voice is special, and always encouraging. More of about hearing God's voice in later testimonies, but for now, let me share one instance of a "Sharp Rebuke from God."

This is not a hallucination, nor is it a delusion, because I am of sound mind, and I know in my inner being that it was real. I was fully awake and conscious sitting in the middle of a church service, the first for the year in fact.

We do not get to hear Him audibly every day, yet God's voice is audible on some special situations. This was one of the situations when it was a direct clear of God as in the voice of a person talking to me, and it took place right in the middle of a church service.

It was the first service and sermon of the year. We were housed in a previous building, where the congregation was smaller, usually between 300-400 people, and the interaction was much more intimate.

I would normally sit in the back row, and this would be about ten to twelve rows back. On that particular morning, I decided to moved up front and ended up just one row behind the front row, with the preacher towards my right side.

Coincidentally, the message was focused on the church's plan to follow the book "Hearing God" by Reverend Henry Blackaby. It was about 15 years ago, and I had already heard God's voice a few times. At times, I am also able to differentiate the different voices of the Holy Trinity, whether our Father, our Lord Jesus or the Holy Spirit speaking.

I have always noted that the Holy Spirit's voice to be soft and gentle, and messages short and sweet, abrupt at times and in short phrases. Our Heavenly Father would usually address me as son, whereas my Lord Jesus words spoken are often like that between friends.

My attitude was a bit cool, when the senior lady pastor was sharing on the year's commitment to study the book; it was for the whole congregation, so that we can begin to walk closer to God and hear His Voice.

Out of the blue, while Pastor was speaking about the year's plans, I heard an audible voice directed at me:

"My daughter is suffering tremendously under you!"

It hit me like a 'thunderbolt' right in my chest. What a shocking experience it was to me, because I knew in my heart that the LORD was talking to me directly. It was a rebuke, and a direct one too.

I was filled with a lot of guilt and deep remorse simultaneously, and my heart and mind froze then and there during the sermon. I could no longer focus at the message, yet did not go out, as it would have been awkward or misunderstood for me to leave the service half-way.

I held on for the rest of the message, suppressed my emotions for perhaps another 30 minutes.

As soon, as the service ended, I got up and went straight to the carpark where my car was parked. I opened the door, sat down, started the engine, and immediately literally "wept & wept."

Anyone would have done the same, if you had just been rebuked by the LORD. He had called my wife "her daughter".

I have often reflected back at the incident and equated it to a trip back to your wife's family after a while, and at the door, your father-in-law greets you with this rebuke:

"What have you done to my daughter!"

It was either that I am guilty of doing wrong, or that I have not done right. I was responsible for the state she was in and it was time for me to do something about it to rectify it.

I was saved by grace in 1981, and since then until that incident (around 2004), my beloved wife had not yet come to the saving knowledge of Jesus. It has been tough for both parties, and a lot of misunderstandings and differences have resulted.

Perhaps, the season of January 2004 was the peak of all that we have gone through. It has been another fifteen years since, and perhaps it is yet another reminder to me to "look after my Father's daughter better".

What have I learned from this testimony?

A soft rebuke from the LORD is very scary. Imagine His booming sound that the Israelis heard when Moses came down from Mount Sinai.

Let us not take God's grace for granted.

Testimony # 039   Holy Spirit spoke: "Read Proverbs 6"

Still on the theme of God's voice, this testimony is about the voice of the Holy Spirit, who dwells in us.

This took place while I was serving in Kuala Terengganu, and East Coast town, where my wife was born. It was around 1990 or 1991, when again, out of the blue, God spoke to me in a still small voice: "Read Proverbs 6."

I didn't think much of it when I heard it that day. On the next day, the same still small voice spoke again: ***Read Proverbs 6,*** this time more emphatic, and a clear reminder that it was a nudge from God to read Proverbs Chapter 6. It was the Holy Spirit.

The voice was soft, clear, gentle but firm, and just audible, but clearly authoritative and a directive. I had to obey. So, I picked up my Bible and searched for Proverbs 6. This was the days before the smartphone, and we would need to check our physical Bibles, which I still do when looking for verses.

I read the verses noted down in Proverbs 6.

Proverbs 6:

"My son, if you become surety for your friend,
If you have shaken hands in pledge for a stranger,
You are snared by the words of your mouth;
So, do this my son, and deliver yourself;
For you have come into the hand of your friend:
Go and humble yourself;
Plead with your friend.
Give no sleep to your eyes,
Nor slumber to your eyelids.
Deliver yourself like a gazelle from the hand of the hunter,
And like a bird from the hand of the fowler."

I stopped there as I knew those were the verses meant for me, the first six verses. I paused, was amazed and wondered: "Wow, Proverbs 6! But what has that got to do with me, LORD?" I asked with simple innocence. I read Proverbs 6 again the next day, and asked again, "LORD, I do not understand. What has Proverbs 6 got to do with me? I have not stood as guarantor for anybody."

I continued on with my daily routine and work as usual. Then, on the second day after I had read Proverbs 6, the answer came within me: "Bingo!"

The Holy Spirit revealed to me and gave me the understanding and significance of Proverbs 6 in my life. It began with an image, then the memories came back and unfolded, and the truth hit me like a thunderbolt.

I had been saying to the LORD that Proverbs 6 has nothing to do with me, as I have never given my pledge or guarantee to anyone, and I could not see the relevance of Proverbs 6 in my life.

But it was central to the struggles I was going through, and have been going through now for nearly four decades: 'an unsaved spouse'. God, our Father knows all, remembers all, as He was there at the scene and site. This is what it was:

My wife and I Jane, also a doctor were married in September 1978, after a four-year courtship. We were both non-believers then, and our parents followed a mixture of traditional Chinese belief in Taoism, ancestral worship and Buddhism, with some deity worship mixed in.

Three years after my marriage, I came into the wondrous saving Grace of Jesus Christ, as related in my testimony # 056 'How I Found God'. It was shocking news to my wife and my in-laws when I became a Christian, particularly my mother-in-law.

They were Buddhist-Taoist from the east coast state of Terengganu, and Christianity was not only foreign to them, but considered a no-no, almost like an 'abomination'. In other words, in some cultures in the world, particularly the traditional ones, Christianity is considered an outcast religion. I recently heard from a man of God the same views in traditional India, where social class is still strongly followed that Christians were considered of a low class, and deserved to be served last in the early days.

My beloved mother-in-law was very upset that I had made that decision to embrace a new faith, and she expressed her disappointment by saying that "if she knew I was going to become a Christian, she would not let me marry her daughter". That was how extreme the position and opinion at that time and even up to this moment with my in-laws. I was now an 'outcast' in some of their eyes.

"Kim Hock (my Chinese name) has become a Christian!"

Soon after my return to Kuala Lumpur, I made plans to go back to the United Kingdom to complete my training as well as take the examinations for postgraduate studies to become a specialist in internal medicine. My first attempt at the examinations did not succeed. My wife, Jane and daughter Grace, then barely 4 months were to come along.

I still recall vividly, at the sendoff at the Subang International Airport in Kuala Lumpur, just before the boarding for the flight, my mother-in-law approached me directly and said, "Promise me that you will not convert Jane to Christianity."

It was a direct request, almost as good as an instruction, which I could not directly reject. Out of politeness and respect, I looked at her, smiled and kind of nodded my head in half agreement. **That was the binding agreement, promise or guarantee that the Holy Spirit was telling me about through Proverbs 6.**

As much as an "amen" is powerful and effective, apparently that "nod' was a form of "guarantee" that was obstructive to the working of the "Good News" on my precious beloved. Such an agreement was binding, sufficient to nullify attempts to share the Gospel to this beloved, because of the words of my mouth.

What a powerful revelation from the LORD to me. I had to do it. I had to break the binding vow that I had made some 15 years prior. Proverbs 6 was suddenly relevant to me with such clarity and conviction. It was the LORD. No doubt at all in my mind at all. I was not familiar with the contents of Proverbs 6 before this, although I have read it before. Also, the words: "Read Proverbs 6" came out of the blue and was repeated the following day.

'Proverbs 6' spoke with a sense of urgency that it was necessary to get my release from a vow: "Do not wait!" This meant that I had to act as soon as possible. It was a temporarily relief that my mother-in-law was out of town, and would only be back in a week. Naturally, I was nervous, and with some trepidation about how to go about it; yet I knew that there was no other way out but to obey and face the risk of a confrontation.

On her return, over the first two days, I could not sum up enough courage to ask her. It was perhaps on third day of her return that I felt that the moment had arrived. I had to do it that day.

Before anyone thinks otherwise, my relationship with my in-laws are good and cordial and there has never been a misunderstanding over the years, except for that statement that she was not pleased about my faith. In fact, the discovery of my new faith took place over a meal, when I declared that I could not eat the food that was offered to idols. That first instance had provoked displeasure and unhappiness, but subsequently it was resolved amicably and mother-in-law, who is a great cook, would herself inform me that this section was food offered to idols and the other section was free for me to eat.

It was the routine then for family members to gather in my home, and have dinner almost nightly. After dinner, they would take a rest or nap before heading off home, to their own home, which was about fifteen minutes by car.

On that particular night, the routine was the same. After dinner, they rested and it was around 11 p.m. that they left. Somehow, I did not have the courage to bring the matter up, but as I had felt the need to settle it that night, I picked up the telephone at about 11.40 p.m. and called home to speak to my mother-in-law. This was during the days before the mobile phone was freely available.

My sister-in-law picked the phone and passed it to mother-in-law.

I said, "Mum, hi mum. Sorry to call so late, but I had meant to bring it up a moment ago, but did not find the suitable moment. Well, I would like to talk about the time you spoke to me about...."

I had hardly completed the sentence when she reacted sharply, as if she knew what the issue was: "What is the matter?"

I could hear her tell my sister-in-law after that, "Let's go down!"

I immediately said in a calm tone, "No need, mum. No need to come over"

I continued directly to the point, "All I ask is for you to release me of that pledge, which you asked from me, more than ten years ago. You asked me to promise not to convert Jane to Christianity."

Jane heard the conversation and was annoyed that I was probing her mum at this time on this matter, and she declared that she was not going to be 'so foolish' to follow me.

Caught between the cross fire of wife and mother-in-law, I could only pray silently, as time seemingly froze for a few seconds.

Suddenly, to my surprise and unexpectedly, over the phone, amidst the commotion and confusion, mother declared: "Well, it's up to her. It's up to her!"

Wow, praise God! With that word, I got the release, and was free from the pledge. Hallelujah!!

"Thank you mum, good night" I whispered in relief and put the phone down. I looked up at the clock, and it was past midnight.

What a drama! Proverbs 6. God has spoken, and I had obeyed, and the vow was nullified.

A new chapter had begun.

What have I learned from this testimony?

When THE LORD speaks, it is definitely a divine guidance, and this advice allowed me to have a spiritual breakthrough in being released from a binding vow. The Holy Spirit opened my eyes to understand and act correctly.

If you have a deadlock, a difficult problem, seek God's help, ask Him to reveal to you the solution: "Speak to me, LORD; answer when I call."

He will do so for you as He did to me, showing me that I had to be released from my vow. Read the next testimony which is another example in my life.

Testimony # 040 "The Photograph"

This happened around the end of 1985. I had just returned from my second trip to the United Kingdom, after having completed my postgraduate training and studies in Neurology, a subspecialty involving diseases of the brain and the nerves.

I recall that I was impacted by the last message by my Pastor from Elim Pentecostal church on the need to be baptized in the Holy Spirit. Hitherto, I was high in my faith, sailing along happily, with Jesus as my Lord and Savior.

Then, came along this teaching and concept that was following the Charismatic movement then, about the Baptism of the Holy Spirit and the speaking in tongues.

It was foreign to me. Yet, I was still seeking for more and more. Over the first four years of my salvation, I had given up to as many as eight testimonies in church on how I came to know Jesus. A lot of people were blessed to hear about my journey seeking the GOD and finding Jesus as Savior.

I thus started on the next journey to seek more from God, to seek the baptism of the Holy Spirit and to speak in tongues. From my own search in the Revised Standard Version or RSV as it was popularly called, out of the five times, 'baptism of the Holy Spirit' was referred to in four occasions, it was followed by manifestation of tongues, and fire, while in one, the individual was filled with joy.

I was truly genuinely searching. It so happened, that the subsequent messages around that time did involve the baptism of the Holy Spirit.

The first time I sought the baptism of the Holy Spirit was with an elder in my church, who laid hands on me, and prayed. Nothing happened.

Then, there were visiting speakers, many of whom are anointed to pray for baptism of the Holy Spirit. Two of them came by and I went forward to be prayed for. The first three altar-based prayers did not produce any manifestations, nor did I feel anything.

To me, it was odd or serious, as this should not be so, considering that I had made attempts to search for the truth, and to receive the anointing and baptism.

I then felt the need to seek THE LORD, which I did. I went on my knees and sought the LORD. "LORD, why LORD? What is the obstacle? Is there any reason for this inability to be released in tongues, to receive the full baptism of the Holy Spirit?"

I prayed and waited.

About two days later, I heard two words: "The Photograph!"

The photograph? What does it mean? I don't understand? What photograph?

As I posed and asked this question, it took less than a day when 'the photograph' concerned flashed in my mind. I looked into the pile of photographs and I found it.

It was a wedding photograph. My wife and I were kneeling before an altar of a popular lady Chinese deity, as a prayer in our marriage. I picked up the photo and looked at the back of it and was shocked with what had been written, about seven years prior. It was a promise and pledge before that deity.

Imagine that I had already forgotten about that act or incident, and also had the impression that once I had made a pledge to follow Jesus, all these past things did not matter anymore. While that is true, in my opinion, 'the evidence' remains damaging and the 'enemy' can still use these points to frustrate us, as false accusation and attacks are a common 'modus operandi' in spiritual warfare.

I was relieved that I took the necessary action, and felt the peace. Within the next day or so, I heard two more words: 'The negatives!'

What? The negatives? This was in the days of film photography, and it was a common practice to keep the negatives so that we can reprint the photos when needed.

I obediently follow, and found the negatives, and dutifully destroyed them.

I was free.

From there, I proceeded, and with the next anointed man of God, I went forward to the altar for prayer. Nothing happened on the fourth and fifth prayer until the sixth prayer and laying of hands. One Reverend Francis from Singapore prayed, and gave a little push to my belly, and then 'tongues' were released and spoken from my lips.

Praise God! I was finally baptized in the Holy Spirit. At a later date, I was to receive activation of various kinds of tongues. Testimony # 058.

It is tough for a neurologist and many men and women, who think a lot to suppress the mind and allow faith and the baptism of the Holy Spirit to work. One has to be humble and yearn for the things of God, and more of God to step forward in the spiritual realm.

What have I learned from this testimony?

An object, a photograph was an obstacle to my spiritual growth; the incriminating photograph, which I had forgotten about was the obstacle that the accuser used to block me from receiving the Baptism of the Holy Spirit. Once that was dealt with, the Courts in Heaven closed my file, and I was filled with the Holy Spirit and released in tongues.

Testimony # 041 "You Shouldn't Pray Like That!"

This is the fourth testimony in this series on 'hearing from God', all of which, I believe is the Holy Spirit speaking to me.

It was a Chinese New Year eve. There is a popular practice that is still going on until today, when celebrants will set off firecrackers just after midnight to usher in the Chinese New Year.

The Chinese New Year is the biggest, busiest and most grand celebration of the year for the Chinese in Malaysia. The setting of firecrackers is a big part of these celebrations, which run on for at least fifteen days into the New Year.

This was in the year 1987 or so, when my two children then were ages one and five. They had gone to bed and were sleeping peacefully. I was very worried that they would be awakened by the loud blasts of the firecrackers, which would start on the dot at midnight.

I positioned myself in their rooms at around 11.45 p.m. just in case they were woken up, and I started to pray, especially praying in tongues. Just as soon as the clock struck twelve, at midnight, the firecrackers began to blast away. I prayed fervently in tongues, and my two children slept peacefully past the first five to ten minutes.

I continued to pray onwards, as they slept peacefully. My prayers were working. Then suddenly, around 10-15 minutes past midnight, while the firecrackers were loudly blasting away and I was praying in tongues, I heard a clear voice directly towards me.

"You shouldn't pray like that!"

"What?! I shouldn't pray like that? I am praying in tongues," I replied to the Holy Spirit.

I continued to pray, and then the Holy Spirit opened my eyes in answer to my queries.

What had happened was that, I was now into my 5th year as a believer, and we, together with Grace my daughter had made two trips to the United Kingdom and had stayed there now for two years in all.

Yet, my beloved wife Jane was still nowhere near the faith, and in fact the inter-faith tensions as I call it, was getting worse and worse. We had issues about my children, aged one and five and we could not agree about them following me to church. I was also hardly involved in the church, except for attending the Sunday morning service.

In my frustration then, I had said a horrible prayer, about three months prior. It is a prayer that I have repented on, and am too ashamed to repeat here in print.

What an awful and brutal, if not deadly prayer, even if I meant well.

After that prayer, for the next three months, as I had prayed, we had 'hell'! We were at each other's throats at loggerheads day and night, often until as late as 2 a.m. squabbling away. Effectively, after that prayer, there was no peace in my home.

I recall one particularly night when we were literally exhausted, when I remarked, "Darling, let's go to sleep; we are working tomorrow. And it was 2 a.m. already. The answer came, "I do not care."

That was the 'nasty' prayer that I had made, and the very prayer that resulted in a rebuke from the Holy Spirit, i.e. "You shouldn't pray like that!"

I immediately repented. And, it was the eve of the Chinese New Year.

My two children slept peacefully. I recall that particular Chinese New Year, as we had invited guests, and hence were busy at work till 3 a.m. preparing the home for guests, while simultaneously quarreling!

I recall very vividly, that following my repentance and retraction of my nasty request, peace slowly came in as the quarrels simmered down, and by the fifth day after I repented, peace returned.

What have I learned from this episode?

From this and the two-month story to Holland, and the pen stories, I am now utterly convinced that we are so powerful in our prayers, and the desires of our hearts, that we must indeed be very careful, as to what we want and what our hearts desire.

Testimony # 042 "When I asked ABBA Father"

Hearing God's voice matters a lot. Jesus said in John 10:27, "My sheep hear My voice, and I know them, and they follow Me.

From my personal experience, perhaps for half of the times that God has spoken, it was in as a result of my questions. God answers us when we ask. Try it and you will begin to hear God speak.

This testimony is about my second child, John who was about six years of age then, and ready to enter primary school. Grace, my eldest child is about five years older, and she had been enrolled into a public school throughout her studies.

We were discussing as a family as to where we should put John, either in a public school or in a private schooling system. In the early nineties, private schools were beginning to flourish in Malaysia and more and more parents were placing their children in private schools. Currently, of course, the first choice for most parents and children is private schooling.

The two kids, Grace then about ten or eleven and John just six were discussing, with Grace for the public system and John being open to the private system. My wife and I were of course very keen to try out the private schooling system.

When kids 'quarrel', parents often come up with a wise answer. Mine came suddenly, and I blurted out.

"Stop quarreling. Daddy will ask the LORD."

It all went quiet. John, just six took it literally and in full faith. Over the next two days, he kept pestering me with the question: "What did the LORD say?"

"Dad, what did the LORD say?"

On the third day, just as I was entering the kitchen, John asked the same question again. I said, "Wait…."

Then, I told the LORD, "LORD, surely you must answer me. Should we send John to public or private schooling?"

Within seconds the answer came, as He spoke, "Son, I grant you the desires of your heart."

Yeah! I heard it. He has approved my desire to send John to the private schooling system. That's the answer. Those were my thoughts, just before He spoke again.

Interestingly, and indeed God's sense of humor, followed, as after the pause, He continued, "Even if I told you, you would not have followed Me."

Wow! That was a gentle rebuke. The LORD meant that if He said "public schooling", I may not have followed.

I didn't think deeply over those words, but immediately told John and Grace, "It's private system."

Interestingly, after five years in the private system, we felt it was a wrong decision, and made an application back to the public system. It was a year of testing and trial for John, as he switched to a totally different system. It probably unsettled him too much, and we had to bring him back to the private system after a year.

What did I learn from this testimony?

I am more careful when I ask the LORD since then. If He answers, we should obey. In this instance, the LORD was gracious to allow me to choose and decide.

Testimony # 043   Near Collision Averted

There are probably hundreds of times in our lives, that we have near misses, survived and life went on as though nothing happened.

This short testimony relates to one such situation.

I was on the highway during a time when there was no divider in this particular stretch of highway. This means that both sides are travelling at fairly high speed and overtaking around bends can be dangerous. As a rule, if there are double lines dividing the road, it indicates that overtaking is not allowed.

It was a relatively straight road with my family heading towards the East Coast of Peninsular Malaysia, when I suddenly heard an exploding sound, similar to that of a burst tire in the distance. Next, in a distance, I saw the lights of a lorry being switched on, and then to my 'horror', I saw the lorry heading towards my car.

The whole situation probably lasted 5-10 seconds at the most, but I can still replay it in my mind, in slow motion.

I instantly knew that something was wrong, and that the lorry was veering towards me, and it must have had a burst tire, and the driver had turned on the lights to warn oncoming cars.

In that two or three seconds, racing in my mind was, "what should I do?" Accelerate and drive faster or slow down and even brake. When in doubt, I am one of those guys who will do nothing.

Thus, I did nothing, but cruised along at the same speed. I was thinking quite fast though. If I accelerated, I might have actually entered the path of the lorry, and if I had slowed down, I may end up being a direct target of the straying vehicle.

In actual fact, I was a helpless observer, watching the lorry veer into my path. Just about 50 meters from my car, the lorry suddenly changed course and moved past me.

It is interesting that during that period of barely 10 seconds, there was little time to think, little time to pray, but just being frozen and trusting the LORD.

I thank God that yet again, a near collision or accident was averted just in time.

I thank God that my angels, and special extra angels came by to save me and my family.

What did I learn from this incident?

Praying for safety and mercy journey is important. My daughter always prays Psalm 91 protection whenever any of us travel. Psalm 91 has only 16 verses, and is certainly worth remembering and memorizing. "The LORD is my refuge and my fortress...in Him I will trust. He shall deliver me from the snare of the fowler... from the perilous pestilence. under His wings... be my shield and buckler... I shall not be afraid of the terror by night, nor of the arrow by day. nor pestilence in darkness. a thousand may fall. ten thousand. but it shall

not come near me. no evil shall befall me. nor any plague near my dwelling… for He shall give His angels charge over me… they shall bear me up. I shall tread upon the lion and the cobra. "

Powerfully, "The LORD will be with me in trouble, deliver me, and honor me, and with long life, He will satisfy me. and show me His Salvation.

Testimony # 044   Burst Tire Averted

This is yet another testimony of a disaster averted.

I was driving a smaller economical car, a Honda City, with Good Year tires, and the mileage was probably about 20 thousand kilometers. I normally can run up to 40 thousand kilometers on my tires. The thread was still good, and I use this car only for drives within the city.

For that particular two weeks, I had felt a little wobbly when I turned the car during short turns. However, on the road, it all seemed fine.

My classmate passed away that week, and I wanted to drive down to Malacca, about 200 kilometers away with the same car, something I have never done with this same car.

My dear wife, in her wisdom discouraged me and the trip was cancelled. That probably averted a burst tire. Little did I know that the right rear tire had bulged on the inner side, and would probably had burst on a long drive. It was in fact the size of a mango or about 6 inches by four inches in dimension.

A day or so later, while I was driving along the road, another driver kept pointing to my car, to alert me that something was not in order. I immediately dutifully drove to the side and looked all-round the car and found nothing wrong, and drove off again.

On that weekend, I happened to be moving office, and there was a small lorry carrying my stuff, while I drove in front to lead the way. The thought came to me that they could see my tires. I called the driver and asked him if he saw anything untoward about my car.

The lorry driver told me as he was following me, that there was something stuck to my tires, perhaps some sticky paper or something like that. I still did not feel anything wrong while driving, though I did not drive fast.

We moved my stuff into my new office. It was after that when I paused and took a good look at my tires.

To my shock and horror, I saw a big bulge measuring about 6 by 4 inches, like a big mango extruding from the side of the tire. It was clear that it was about to burst through any time. I have never seen such a phenomenon before. I immediately changed the tire and asked my regular supplier to send it back to the manufacturers with a complaint.

The tire man affirmed that the tire most likely would have burst on a long trip on the high way. The LORD had protected me once again.

What do I learn from this episode?

We often take it lightly when we have a near miss. If only we are able to see what disaster we missed, the danger involved and how the LORD through His angels protected us from harm. I thank the LORD for yet another situation where He is my Protector.

Pray and receive Psalm 91 over our lives.

Testimony # 045   Safe Landing on 8th Attempt

All of us who fly would have had some experience we they sensed danger, or there was potential danger in the air. This testimony is a short one about one rare situation where the airplane we were in could not land.

We were flying from the East Coast town of Kuala Terengganu, heading towards Kuala Lumpur, and about to land in the KLIA 1, or Kuala Lumpur International Airport Number One, when we experienced heavy thunderstorm and rain.

The airplane could not land, because of the adverse conditions. I was interestingly seated beside a Muslim fellow passenger. We were chatting away as the plane approached the runaway and went past towards the Straits of Malacca, as we saw the large space of water beneath.

The pilot or captain did not say anything, but it was obvious. We approached land for the first time and just before the coastline, the airplane made a U-turn and went back towards the Straits.

This went on the second, third, fourth, fifth and sixth failed landing, hence getting ready for the seventh attempt to land, I was getting worried, and turned to my Muslim co-passenger and said, "Let us pray for a safe landing."

Most Muslims from the East Coast State of Terengganu are prayerful people, and the State is known as the Land of Faith.

We stopped talking and started praying quietly on our own. We were already about twenty minutes in the air, trying to land. If the airplane could not land, we would be diverted to either

Penang or Johor Bahru, which would be another 40 minutes away. The seventh approach was not successful, as the pilot did an eighth U – turn back to the expanse of water.

I had two concerns as a lay person. One was whether there would be enough gasoline, just in case there was bad weather in the other airport. The second, of course, as with any traveler was the inconvenience caused by a considerable delay of having to fly back again when the weather was better.

We visibly and almost audibly stepped up our prayer as we approached the runway for the 8th time, and the plane landed safely amidst the heavy rain.

Normally, the Malaysian weather, when it pours 'cats and dogs' it will go on for easily for an hour, but in this instance, it did abate in less than that for the plane to land.

As we walked into the airport, with wind and water still gushing down, we were greeted by various aircrew staff who told us, "You are 'lucky' to be able to land. The other planes were diverted to Penang."

We were the first to land in that storm.

I believe prayer.

What can I say but to give thanks every time and all the time for His goodness?

Prayer is powerful. The effective and fervent prayer of a righteous man avails much. James 5:16. Thus, the key is to stay righteous and to be fervent and effective in prayer.

Testimony # 046   Possessed Live-in Maid

This was during the time when we were working in Sarawak, Borneo in the late eighties, and the incident happened around 1983.

Grace was about two years in age, and my wife Jane, was pursuing her postgraduate studies in Pediatrics. We had hired a live-in maid, - a young Iban girl, perhaps about 20 years in age.

Jane had a four weeks clinical attachment in Singapore in a good center for Pediatrics. I was left alone with the maid and my two-year old daughter. On retrospect, it was probably not a good arrangement. We were young and had full trust in each other, and society at that time was less 'suspicious'. She was 'Christian' from a Protestant denomination, and we were attending an evangelical church called SIB Church, in Iris Garden, Kuching.

Out of the blue, one evening, she began to complain of a severe throbbing headache, and became very anxious and restless, and nearly berserk.

Sensing that things were not right, I was firm and asked her directly what was wrong with her, as her behavior was odd.

Over the years, I have come to realize the awesome authority in us, given to us from the time of Adam, to subdue and dominate or rule the earth. Thus, when I enquired, as to what was wrong, "she had to tell me."

She related that since she was young, a spirit couple had come into her life, and took control her, giving her instructions from time to time. Apparently, when she almost died when she was an infant, and her grandmother then had invoked some spirits and given her to them as her guardians. She called these spirit couple her 'parents', and they would visit her nightly. They have in fact ordered her not to tell anyone about this relationship, and even her parents are not aware of it. In her village, the spirit couple had instructed her to build an altar in a hidden place where she would worship them. If she did not obey or comply, they would often discipline her and hit her on the head causing her to have headaches.

Obviously, they had followed her to my house. At midnight, that night after this story was revealed to me, they came, and Junie (not her real name) would cry and the dogs outside would howl.

It was a clear manifestation. I believe because of my position and authority as a believer, it was not compatible with this maid living in my house, and the spirits were not pleased with that.

I called for help, and a sister from the church, a fellow Iban girl Melanie, in her late twenties came over and stayed for the night. I decided to bring Junie for deliverance the next day, with her permission, of course. After the church service, we arranged for a deliverance prayer session in another church, where brother Henry and Donald were worshipping. These two young men, like Daniel and his friends were gifted in able to see and pray for deliverance.

We worshipped the LORD, sang and praised and prayed for deliverance. This went on for an hour with no results.

Henry saw six demons inside. None moved as all refused to leave. We stopped and one of the brothers counselled Junie to confess and say the sinner's prayer and declare Jesus is Lord of her life. Softly and clearly, she said the prayer, probably sincerely too for the first time, as we were to discover later. As soon as she said the prayer, all the demons fled, and she was delivered!

It was a joyous moment, and we continued to praise the LORD and worship for several minutes after that.

After that prayer, Junie confessed that although she was regularly attending church, she had not confessed about this relationship with the spirits and she had not yet cut them off, until that afternoon. We had a joyous celebration together over lunch.

Henry told us that these spirits may return again. That evening, at about 6.30 p.m., the spirits returned and were around my house. I could not see them, but Junie knew and was disturbed. I called for help, and Henry came with his guitar, with Melanie still around.

We sang praises. Henry saw a group of demons approaching and when we sang praises, an army of angels came and formed an outer circle and the demons fled. Hallelujah, Praise the LORD! God is our deliverer.

What have I learned from this testimony?

The spirit realm is real and active. We may not see, hear or feel, but there are ongoing activities in the air. Prayers matter, and regular prayer and trust in the LORD will diminish and minimize such disturbances in our lives.

Testimony # 047   Ghost Family in the House

This happened to a close relative's family.

About a few years back, I called on this close relative and asked him to bring his family over to my office for a chat. He came along with his wife and two lovely girls, whom I shall refer to as Kit and Lian. Kit was about twelve and Lian eight.

The purpose of that visit was clear. I wanted to share the Good News about Jesus to them, as there were various issues in the family. I was direct and shared freely about the love of Jesus, and how knowing Him would change and transform their lives. It was a short sharing that lasted perhaps about 30 minutes, including the usual greetings and social chat.

When it ended, he and family was about to leave, when he thanked me for my love and concern for him and his family. He then said something strange.

"Uncle, I want to tell you that there is another family staying with us?"

"What do you mean?" I asked.

"There is a ghost family staying with us for the past seven years. We (me and my wife) cannot see them, but Kit and Lian can. In fact, Lian calls them Cheh-cheh's friend as Kit knew them earlier." (Cheh-cheh means 'sister' in Cantonese)

When I heard that, I told him and his family that we should not let that unhealthy situation continue. The wife chipped in to say that of late, they have begun to see and hear strange things like the door knob handle turning.

"In this case, there is an urgency for all of you as a family to come to know and receive Jesus as your Savior and Lord. He will protect you. When you receive Him as your Savior, the spirits will leave," I declared.

They agreed. We bowed our heads, as I led them as a family to confess that Jesus is Lord, and Son of God and to welcome and accept Him as our personal Savior, followed by a prayer for the forgiveness of sins.

All of them, including Kit and Lian clearly followed in the prayer. It was a joyful time, as one family was ushered into the Kingdom of God. I followed by praying for the family, and declaring that they now belonged to Jesus, and rebuking the spirit family and telling them to leave in Jesus Name.

I then advised them that the spirit family may return and if they did, just pray and declare that "Jesus is LORD!"

They then left my office.

That night, at about 2 a.m., the spirits returned and Kit was restless, crying and disturbed. Her father rushed to the bedside, and remembered my advice, and proceeded to urge Kit to pray.

"Kit, pray, Kit pray. Say Jesus is LORD. Say Jesus is LORD."

Kit, in her weepy, half asleep state tried, and out came some 'gibberish' words.

The father continued to urge her on to say that 'Jesus is LORD'. After several minutes of struggling for words, Kit finally garnered enough strength, opened her mouth and softly uttered: "Jesus, Jesus. Jesus is Lord."

Almost at that instant, according to the father, peace came the home, and the demons have never returned since.

Subsequently, a cell group have visited the home and prayed for deliverance and covering. I have also made one visit to this particular home.

The young family have joined a neighboring church and cell and are growing in their faith.

I have shared this story and this testimony a few times since. What is so awesome about this story is the power in the Name of Jesus, and the faith of a little girl.

A twelve-year-old girl, barely 12 hours in her faith in knowing Jesus, calling upon the awesome and mighty name of Jesus, could chase away a family of demons who have been there in their home for seven years.

What is so powerful about this testimony?

The Name of the LORD is awesome and powerful. The demons tremble at His Name, and at the Name of Jesus, they flee. For that reason, we must not take His Name in vain.

Testimony # 048   Headaches from Spirit Attacks

These two situations are just among the many times when my patients have suffered from these unseen forces.

One was a Chinese lady, single and in her early forties. She was seeing me for headaches for over a year, and had also been receive various forms of treatment for her so-called migraine attacks. She also had a course of Botulinum toxin injection by another doctor, with little improvement.

On this visit to see me about fifteen years ago, she related to me her agonizing headaches that had been troubling her for some months then. I reassured her that everything was all right and her brain scans were normal.

She then related to me what was happening in her home situation. She said that she and her brother owned a two-room apartment. They had let it out for a season, and had now taken it back. Since they moved back into their own apartment, they have been having severe headaches.

When they moved in, they tried sleeping in their rooms, but felt a strong oppression, and their heads were throbbing. They could also hear voices telling them to get out of the room. As a result, both siblings had to endure sleeping in the sitting hall in their own apartment.

I gave a very simple advice and asked her whose apartment it was, and taught this lady (a Catholic) to claim the apartment back in the Name of Jesus, and to take authority to rebuke the spirits to leave, as they were the rightful owners of that place.

Her headaches improved after that.

In the second case, this family lived next to the Highland Towers in Ampang. The tower had collapsed and dozens of people in it had perished. After the collapse, apparently the family members saw apparitions walking around their home, some headless, some without limbs. Each member of the family was falling sick one by one, and visitors to their home too began to fall sick. It could have been a coincidence, but one relative from abroad came over stayed, fell very sick and passed away. Even a neighbor who had dropped by to visit had suffered a heart attack and died.

This patient suffered relentless headaches for over four years.

They decided to move out of their home, and these apparitions followed them. In desperation, they hired over a dozen traditional spiritual practitioners or 'Bomohs' and it made things worse. There were instances when they opened the front door in the morning, they saw eggs or sand or even small knives or swords on the pathway, even with their faces imprinted on the eggs.

I asked her two questions. One was whether she was the owner of the house and she replied "Yes." The second was whether she had robbed a bank or killed someone. Both answers were a clear, "No!"

As she was Muslim, I decided to give her some generic advice. I said, since this is your property and you are a good person, this is how you should pray and declare.

"Almighty God, I declare before You, that this is my house. I am a good person, and have not killed anyone or robbed anyone. I therefore speak with authority to all those spirits around here to leave this place as this place belongs to me and my family."

That was all she did. I called her a few days later, and asked her how things were at home. She replied, that things were much better, and the disturbance much less.

"Thank you, LORD."

What did I learn from this episode?

It is all about ownership and authority. Even the spiritual realm has to obey authority. When we believe in Jesus, the powerful Spirit of Christ is in us.
[Romans 8:9 Now if anyone does not have the Spirit of Christ, he is not His.]

Testimony # 049   Oppressed for Three Months

This happened in the mid-eighties, when I was a relatively young Christian, barely 3 or 4 years into the faith.

I was feeling 'under the weather' for a period of over three months, not really sure what was wrong. It was a time when my mood was down, and zest also flat and although I could continue with the daily routine of work and family, I was not in top form.

Little did I know till later that I was actually being `oppressed or harassed'.

We were having a short prayer meeting among the three of us doctors, Dr Thomas and Dr Mapphy at the former's office, one mid-week afternoon, when we decided to have a short time of prayer. I had not said anything, and all of us were seemingly well on the outside.

As soon as we entered prayer, Dr Thomas saw a big monkey-like figure, with huge eyes enveloping the arms and legs around me, literally hugging me or holding me in a form of 'embrace'.

He immediately prayed and asked the LORD, what it was. The answer he got was that this is a 'messenger from Satan, sent to harass me, but unable to harm me.' As soon as he received the word, he prayed and rebuked the creature.

At the rebuke, the creature released its grip on me, stood afloat for a moment, looked directly at Thomas and then flew off. Thomas immediately related what he saw and what he heard from the LORD, and what happened after he prayed.

I felt instant peace and a feeling of being light and free, something that seemed missing over the three months prior to that. It was a sort of cloud that had been hanging over me, and that cloud had left.

"Oh, so that was what it was these past three months. I have been feeling low, down and my mood was flat. Thanks Thomas! Thank you, LORD" I said to both Thomas and Mapphy.

I felt happy and relaxed that the 'unseen load' or burden had been lifted up.

I went on normally, until about a few weeks later, when I felt the same sense of heaviness and low feeling in my mood suddenly.

I knew what it was, and said, "In the Name of Jesus, go away!" and I have been all right since.

It has got me wondering whether "Depression", "Malaise", "Discouragement", "Suicide" and many other mental and emotional situations are due to such similar attacks, and 'clouds of gloom' over our lives.

What have I learned from this testimony?

The enemy sends clouds over our lives, and even messengers to harass us. God is my deliverer and protector, and He can deliver us from all forms of oppression.

Testimony # 050   Gold Dusts on my Pants

Before one shuts off one's mind and pooh-pooh about miracles like 'gold dusts' falling, read and hear this testimony. This testimony is true, and witnessed by many of my friends and many pastors who saw the gold dusts on my trousers.

This followed the Lakeland episode, where the 'controversial' minister Todd Bentley was key to the Lakeland revival that went on for several months from April 2008. Two ministers from Malaysia attended the meeting for a week, and brought back the `fire' by conducting a series of daily meetings. My daughter and I attended three or four of these meetings in Kuala Lumpur, a sort of spill-over or spill off from Lakeland.

At one of the meetings, as we prayed and worshipped, gold dusts covered my daughter's hands, and the glittering dusts could be seen clearly. They lasted minutes and then disappeared.

I prayed for it, but nothing happened to me over the next few meetings. Some weeks after that, exactly on the 16th of September 2008, while I was driving, I suddenly noticed that my pants were glittering and filled with gold dusts by the hundreds. I wear black pants almost all the time, and the contrast of gold dusts over dark pants was very striking, especially when one shines a torch light on it. I kept the pants for a total of four years, with hundreds of gold dusts on it. During that time, I showed it to many people, and two ministers gave a prophetic word for me over the incident. Not surprisingly, when I showed it to some men and women of God, they were not interested and preferred not to see the pants.

When one views it under a magnifying glass, with a light shining on it, it looks like beautiful gold nuggets on the fabric. This was demonstrated to many witnesses. I took pictures of it. I was able to transfer it on to paper, and even glass slides and on further analysis, they were opaque, round golden 'nuggets' like objects and they measured only 0.2 mm in diameter. I compared it with commercial decorative gold dusts and those were chunks of a millimeter or more. I did not analyze it chemically though.

I will now describe one phenomenon to show that it was not a fake phenomenon. The pants were kept in a thick yellow plastic bag. Each time a minister came, I offered him or her to sweep their hands in the plastic bag and a few gold dusts will stick to their palms in many cases. In one instant, a fervent business lady from Singapore came to attend a meeting by Chuck Pierce. She put her right hand in and moved it around and on taking it out, the right palm was full of glittering gold dusts.

Just as we were rejoicing at that sight, I noticed that the left palm which did not enter the plastic bag was full of gold dusts, meaning that they did not come from the plastic bag, but were fresh gold dusts.

During this episode after the gold dusts fell on my pants, I experienced two more incidents, one in which both my palms were filled with gold dusts lasting for less than an hour, and another when a lady in black dress came to see me for consultation. As she laid down on the examination couch, I noticed her dress was glittering with gold dusts, and she confirmed it too.

I told her that it was just a phenomenon to encourage her as this was happening to me.

I sought the LORD, to find out why He had showered those gold dusts on me, i.e. my pants. I also simultaneously searched the Internet about gold dusts phenomena and found out many fake Christian ministers using this trick to attract attention to themselves.

The LORD, through the Holy Spirit gave me about eight reasons, among which are as follows:

I prayed and asked for that phenomenon to experience it. Hence God gave me the gold dusts
It was to encourage me and built up my faith
It was to encourage others who saw the gold dusts
It was to show me what gold dusts was like – 0.2 mm in size, unlike the commercial ones, to differentiate from fake gold dusts
It was to tell me that God was pleased with me. It had happened exactly on the day that I did something very special for the LORD, which I may share on another page.
It confirms that God can perform miracles for those who believe
 God was telling me that more miracles will take place in my life
It was a testimony that many Godly people still do not believe in miracles

This incident has stepped up my faith to another level, that miracles can happen when we ask and believe.

What do I learn from this testimony?

God is a God of miracles. The manifestation of this miracle experienced by me personally has indeed encouraged, edified and strengthened me spiritual towards greater heights.
I fully agree that miracles may not be the main way to persuade people to Christ, but it is a way, and we cannot forget how Nicodemus, a senior Council member of the Synagogue was moved to believe in Jesus, because of the works that He did.

Testimony # 051   I saw Manna Fall

I had the privilege to witness Harold and Kay Beyer's amazing experience with manna falling over a forty-year period.

As part of their ministry and travel, they visited Kuala Lumpur and ministered in Trinity Community Centre one night.

Again, for those who doubt and are skeptical, this is their testimony that spanned over nearly forty years. They are an ordinary couple, as they testified in their story, written in booklet, by Harold and Kay. Out of the blue, one day, quite similar to my gold dust experience, suddenly

Harold saw flakes of biscuit like fall on his pants and car seat. He was not sure what it was. At home that night, he saw more pieces fall on his Bible and desk. In fact, he was so stunned that he did not dare tell Kay at first.

Over the next few days, it was a daily phenomenon witnessed by both Harold and Kay, with these biscuit-like crumbs falling on his Bible, when he opened the pages of Revelation 2:17, which read:

"To him who overcomes I will give some of the hidden manna to eat."

He took some and ate, and its tasted sweet, like honey, like dried bread or biscuit. Naturally, he and Kay began to share that this phenomenon was happening to them, and those who saw, witnessed and ate the manna were all encouraged.

This went on for some weeks. On one Sunday, while they were seated in one corner of the church, the resident pastor approached them, and told them clearly that what they were doing was not acceptable and they were not welcomed to stay on. That was a clear message that they should leave the church.

That was how the ministry began and it went on for some 38 years, at the time they visited Kuala Lumpur. They were both probably in their late seventies or early eighties when I met them.

I was there with my brother who was then suffering from a terminal cancer. As part of the testimony, they shared that many who partook of the manna had been healed.

While Harold was giving his testimony, fresh manna fell on the page where Revelation 2 was, as it had been happening for the past few decades.

The small congregation of about 150 or so then lined up to having a piece of manna each. The resident pastor was prompted by the Holy Spirit to offer the manna to their own church members, followed by visitors, as he informed me later.

We lined up in a row, giving priority to the members, and then visitors who were unwell. My brother managed to get a piece and partook of the manna, while I was able to take a photo of the manna that had fallen on the page of Revelation in the Bible.

Do I believe in miracles? Yes!

Do I believe it was manna? Yes!

Is Harold and Kay Beyer's testimony real? Yes! Why should they fake it for 40 years?

Can manna still fall? Yes, I believe so. I believe that I may experience it myself too.

I checked on Google on "Manna falling", and discovered that manna has now been falling near the Adventist Mission center in Angola for about forty years too!

God continues to perform miracles every day – only believe.

What do I learn from this testimony?"

Miracles are still happening today, and will continue to happen for those who believe. We can ask God to increase our faith and pray, "LORD, help my unbelief."

Testimony # 052   A Hand fed me Bread

This is a testimony told to me directly by my patient.

She was in her mid-twenties, an Indian Christian girl who was suffering from a severe paralysis of the muscles, affecting of all her arms and legs, and even breathing muscles, an illness called Polymyositis.

She had to be on a ventilator to support her breathing at one time, as her muscles were too weak.

During this episode, she was in a general ward at about midnight. She was too weak to move, and even too weak to call out to the nurses. While she was very hungry one night, she cried out to Jesus, and said, "I am hungry, Lord. I am hungry."

She told me this testimony the next morning, that as soon as she had prayed, almost at an instant, a hand came by her side, and fed her bread. She ate, was satisfied, and went to bed soon after that.

What did I learn from this testimony?

This short and sweet testimony reminds me that our LORD answers prayers instantly and He is never slow. The Hand came to feed her at once.

I am reminded that when we are looking for a car park desperately, The LORD does not tell us to wait till later in the night, when the car park is empty or to come back the next day. He answers our prayers then and there.

Testimony # 053   Babies are from the LORD

While many couples 'worry' about the unexpected pregnancy, there are millions of couples out there longing for a baby, their very precious own child and undergoing all sorts of medical procedures to become pregnant.

For a lot of couples, 'one look' and the wife gets pregnant – a simple peep by one single spermatozoon is enough! For the infertile ones, they pray and cry and faithfully attend fertility clinics for checks, both for man and wife, to try to facilitate fertilization.

Of course, medical science is fantastic, but ultimately, we must believe that fertilization and conception is a miracle, when we consider that the spermatozoa must travel for an equivalent of miles before it reaches the precious and ready ovum.

When we believe that babies are from the LORD, then the key is prayer and belief.

This humble servant has been used by the Almighty for at least four clear occasions, when the respective wives concerned were not able to conceive.

It was a prayer of faith, and like Hannah, all the women were desperate for a child, many for years averaging from 5 to 10 years.

I will relate only one such situation. An Indian lady from the Hindu faith, who had been married for 8 years, and was seeing me for a medical condition, unrelated to the infertility.

I knew that she was married for years and had not yet conceived. They were a lovely couple and were like friends, with a high level of trust between patient, her husband and this doctor.

I offered to pray and declared that 'all babies are from God', and offered to pray in the Name of Jesus for the wife to be able to conceive. We prayed in Jesus Name, and I told them that when she is pregnant, the baby is from Jesus.

A few months later, she ran into my office and wanted to kiss my feet or shoes. I immediately withdrew and said, "No!" Thank the Lord Jesus, for the baby is from Jesus.

There were a few other instances when prayer opened the womb. I was walking along the corridor when I met my optometrist's wife. I asked her why she was here and she said that she had come to tell her husband personally that she was pregnant.

I was surprised that I knew the good news before him. Then she said, "Do you remember that you had prayed for me to have a baby some time ago!" So, not only did she conceive but God allowed it for me to hear the good news before the father of the child!

What did I learn from this testimony?

Faith increases when we exercise faith. I have been praying for many more cases, and can recall four clear cases, and all four will testify that the prayers contributed to their pregnancy.

Testimony # 054   Mates are from the LORD

Isaiah 34:16 is very explicit. The LORD supplies, and arranges a mating partner or a mate for all creatures, from the jackal to the owl, the birds and the beasts in the field. If He so lovingly provides for all these creatures, will He not provide for you too, if you are still single and available.

There is no dating service for all these animals and birds of the air. So, who arranges or finds the mates for each of them? The LORD, Himself, as the Word in Isaiah 34:16 declares.

His promise is clear. "None shall lack a mate."

I only knew about this verse much later after all the situations had taken place.

It began during the time I was leading a Hospital Christian Fellowship in the largest hospital in the country of Malaysia. We were a small group, barely about 8-10 of us. On one meeting, I asked casually whether everyone was married or engaged to be married. All except one sister, in her mid-thirties were married or engaged.

Her name was Joy. Full of faith, I declared that we will pray for Joy for a life partner, to be given to her by the LORD. We prayed and believed and said "Amen."

A short while after that, a young Malaysian man living in London came back and proposed to Joyce, and she is now happily married in London.

Soon after, I asked the same question, and I knew as sister Dr Susan had sadly lost her fiancé about a year or so ago. A wonderful brother has suddenly passed on. It was devastating for her. I asked for permission to pray for her in public and she agreed.

Simultaneously praying for God to comfort her and grant her peace, I prayed that God will give her a new life partner to share her life. Soon after, someone from Brisbane came, and proposed to her and she is now happily married in Brisbane.

I was walking along the corridors of my hospital when one of my nurses casually stopped me with a personal request. She was a charming Pakistani nurse, and about to reach 40 years of age. She appealed to me to "help find for her a life partner, preferably a Malaysian Pakistani Muslim male."

I was frank to answer that it was a difficult task to match make her in Malaysia, but I told her that prayers work, as I have in the past prayed and God had provided a partner for the few I prayed for. I asked her permission to pray for her, and she agreed.

I prayed fervently that God would grant her the desires of her heart and give her a life partner.

A short while after that, a middle-aged widower from Germany, originally from Pakistan visited Malaysia and proposed to her. She is now happily married in Germany.

I bade farewell to my step sister who was moving over to America to serve the LORD. She had a failed marriage in Malaysia. I send her off with a prayer that she would find a man in her life, a partner to journey with her in her walk with the LORD. Soon after, a man of God, a pastor proposed to her. They were married for a few years, but unfortunately, he succumbed to cancer.

After a few years of grieving, God found her another life partner, her third and she is happily married until today.

My daughter and her close friends, all four of them, fervent young female Christians, all attending the same church in Warwick, UK had returned to Malaysia and Singapore, but were still all without any potential life partner. They had all just turned thirty years of age. Like all ladies when they turn thirty, there is a sense of urgency and there was a need to 'pray harder', so to speak for a life partner.

By then, my faith in praying for fertility and a life partner was strong and real, always offering to pray for any lady who needed a life partner. At the same time, my daughter Grace had come across this amazing verse in Isaiah 34:16 that declares that "No one will lack a mate."

I was convinced that if God, our LORD would so assuredly look after the birds and the beasts, even to the point of finding each one a life mate, what more you and I, whom He loves so much.

I happened to be in Singapore at that time, and all the four young ladies had dropped by in the hotel I was staying in. I shared and prayed and we believed and said "Amen" and they each went their way.

It took two to four years when during the same month, three out of four, including my daughter got married, each to the man of their life, as promised by the LORD, and now three of them are blessed mothers.

Hallelujah, praise the LORD!

One out of the four of them, a lovely Singapore girl remains available. I told my daughter Grace that this one, so called left to be single up until now, is so special that the LORD has not forgotten her and has prepared a very special knight of honor for her.

Yes, indeed for all mates are provided by the Good LORD, and we believe and declare His faithfulness for He is the Master Matchmaker.

What have I learned from this testimony?

God takes care of all our needs, from A to Z. In all things, if we ask, seek and knock, we will find. We ask from God; then we need to seek, in whatever way we are comfortable with, which includes meeting people, even going out for healthy, wholesome dates and functions, and finally 'knock' on the hearts of the potential man or woman, by your wooing, radiance, presentation and your personality.

Testimony # 055   Finding Konrad

This testimony happened after God's divine appointment for me and Albert in Perth.

For this trip, I was in Berlin for a few days, and I had specifically wanted to search for an old friend Dr Konrad Brenner. I had previously stayed over in his apartment in 1982 with my wife, Jane and daughter when Grace was an infant.

This time round, Grace was in Britain while I had come over from Kuala Lumpur.

I had misplaced Konrad's number and these was in the days before the smart phone and internet. I had to depend on the telephone directory. I told Grace confidently, that "we will find Uncle Konrad."

However, as hard as I tried, with literally every telephone directory, he could not be found. Yet, I knew that we would find him. On the third day, just when Grace was flying in to Berlin, I asked a German receptionist to look for a Dr Konrad Brenner. "Bingo!" We had a number and I called it, and a familiar German male voice picked up the phone.

We had found Uncle Konrad!

Somehow, the other directories did not have his name there, but this particular one did. We had a wonderful time of reunion together, as we thank God for His faithfulness.

What did I learn from this testimony?

God is so good and faithful and He will direct us along our paths.

Testimony # 056   How I Found God

This is definitely the greatest of all my testimonies. The happiest moment of my life was when I found Jesus, as my LORD and Savior.

It was in 1981, around May when I decided to search for the Living God. I am from a Chinese Buddhist/Taoist background, and having seen and experienced various phenomena in the spirit realm during my childhood and teenage years, it was not difficult for me to believe that there is an Almighty God.

I came to a point when I felt the urge to seek the truth, to know the path towards Almighty God, the Creator to the whole Universe.

I was working as a locum doctor in a 24-hour clinic for extra income. After the crowd had cleared at about 10.30 p.m. in the night, I was free.

A series of thoughts, like questions and answers ran to and fro in my mind. A more detailed story is found in my books, "How I became a Christian" and to be republished as "In Search of The Truth & Beyond."

I felt challenged to start a search for the Living God, and I made the commitment that night to do so. But the question was as to how and in what way I should start. I realized that there were basically three options, if one were to start from square one.

The first was to search on my own, e.g. going to an isolated mountain, or meditate under a tree. I ruled this option out, as I was already a busy trainee doctor, married, and expecting my first child.

The second option would be to find a teacher or guru and learn from him. I quickly discarded this option, as I considered it dangerous and potentially flawed. During that period, there were stories of mass suicide by a cult leader Jim Jones, whose followers were coerced to drink liquid cyanide and all perished in the forests of Guyana. There was also an Indian guru in USA who was famous and rich, and male disciples would be on the streets to sell items to raise funds for him, while the women stayed back to entertain him. I thus ruled out this option too.

I was left with the third and last option, which was to study all the major religions of the world on my own. I decided that I would not let anyone persuade me or prejudice me to follow their faith. I would search the scriptures out myself.

I was convinced that if God is real, surely, I will be able to find God. If God made mankind, surely God must have a path or way for mankind to find God. God could not have made mankind and then abandoned us as a lost species. Would anyone create a big project and then leave it completely? An architect or engineer will always proud of his buildings, so too a doctor who has treated his or her patient successfully, and of course parents, especially the mother who has given birth to her child would be forever linked emotionally, physically and even spiritually to their children.

I was deeply convinced that God can be found and will be found by me, if I embark on a serious search to find God.

On that premise, I accepted that perhaps, one of the major faiths in the world would be correct, and I should read their holy texts, whether the Bible, the Koran, the Bhagavad Gita or Buddhist texts. I was also very clear that I would not be going to church or any place of worship, and would not engage in discussion with anyone of any faith. It was my own personal secret search.

My wife Jane knew that I had embarked on this journey, which in fact was also triggered by her being admitted to hospital for over two months for a threatened labor and enforced bed rest.

All those thoughts happened on that night in May 1981. Two weeks later, I began my search. I went to a Buddhist temple and asked for a holy book, and was told that there was none.

On my shelves, there was a copy of the Holy Bible, based on the Revised Standard Version, a popular version then. I took it, opened it and began my journey reading from the first page from the Book of Genesis.

"In the beginning, God made the heavens and the earth."

What a start! I read with an open mind and with a searching heart and consumed several chapters daily with a voracious appetite for more each day.

It was the first time I had read the Bible or any Holy Book. The stories in the first few books of the Bible were fascinating and engaging.

I began to pray to Almighty God to reveal to me if the Bible was the truth. Somehow, after about two weeks, reading about good kings and evil ones, I decided to prepare my heart, and prayed a prayer of 'repentance' for any sins in my heart so that I could find the Living God.

My daughter, our first child was born about two months after my search began in mid-July, and coincidentally, we named her Grace after an actress not knowing fully at that time what grace meant.

After five months of active daily reading, I completed the Old Testament, and my heart was ready and excited to read the New Testament. It coincided with my travel to the United Kingdom where I was preparing to appear for my postgraduate medical examinations. By then, my heart, mind and soul were literally hungry and ready for the Living God.

God had also put me in a group of friends, most of whom are Christians. We were all appearing for the same postgraduate examinations, and would spend time in discussions on medical topics. It was their practice to pray each time they met. I 'joined' in too, staying in the background.

This was then the first time I was involved with a group of Christians; I broke the news to them that I was searching and had been reading the Bible for about five months.

By that time, I was now reading the Gospels. My friend Chok Wang urged me to attend an evangelistic rally by the late David Watson in Birmingham where we were attached to. I went, and was moved by the message; but I still did not fully believe or accept Jesus as Savior. An elder, Mr. John Cheatle counselled me and prayed for me.

I was alone then in Britain, while wife and baby Grace were in Kuala Lumpur. It was early in my reading of the Gospel of Matthew when I first believed in Jesus, as Lord and Savior of all mankind.

It was the parable of the vineyard that spoke very deeply to my heart, especially in the context of someone who has just freshly read the Old Testament from the first page to the last page of the Book of Malachi.

Here is a God who fully accepts us and welcomes us into His Kingdom, even when we have only just come to believe in Him. It was very natural for me to think that way, while the disgruntled laborers thought otherwise. I understood that once you have become a member of a prestigious club, you are entitled to all the privileges and benefits offered by the club. Once we believe in the Savior, we are ushered as rightful children of God. That was the deep message that spoke to my heart.

Then and then, I believed in my Lord and Savior Jesus and I have not looked back even for a second, over thirty-eight years now.

However, there was a major obstacle. In 1981, the only way I could call home was to go to a special telephone booth meant for international calls, e.g. one situated in Leicester Square. It was not easy and not cheap. We would usually bring a stack of 50 pence coins, as that was the largest denomination available then and accepted by the booth. A stack of 50 pence coins worth about 3-5 pounds sterling would be good enough for a few minutes call only.

How could I call home to explain to my wife that I had come to believe in Jesus, and was going to be a Christian? It was not possible. I decided that I would wait until I got home to Kuala Lumpur, which would be in a few weeks after my examinations. I therefore could not yet accept Jesus as my Savior, although I had already believed.

It was my nightly prayer for the next two weeks. I prayed like this:

"Thank you, LORD, for this amazing journey. I believe in your Son, Jesus, and I believe Jesus is the Savior of the World, who has washed away all the sins of mankind. However, I cannot accept Jesus as my Savior yet, because I have to go back to my country to tell my wife first."

I would then go to sleep after that prayer. This went only for about two weeks every night. I recall reading avidly verses after verses and chapters after chapters of the New Testament till I had reached the Book of Corinthians in two weeks, while still in the United Kingdom.

On the night of the 17th of October 1981, I was sleeping over with my friend Chok Wang, in Lincoln House, East Birmingham Hospital, and it was a Saturday night. I was reading the Book of Corinthians and was about to go to bed at about midnight, when I paused to pray, as I have been doing for some weeks now.

It was the same prayer that I had been saying for over two weeks now. It went again as below:

"Thank you, LORD, for this amazing journey. I believe in your Son, Jesus, and I believe Jesus is the Savior of the World, but…"

I could not proceed with my prayer, stopping abruptly at the word "but". Jesus was knocking on the doors of my heart, pounding away. How could I say, "but I cannot accept you yet", when my Lord Jesus had died on the Cross for me? It was a very lame excuse for me to delay my decision and action to welcome Jesus into my life.

My prayer ended there and then halfway and I decided to go to bed. I lied down, restless, unsettled and feeling remorseful, and torn between the decision to delay or to welcome my Savior into my heart. I tossed and turned as my spirit struggled within me and I could not sleep.

Finally, after about an hour, I sat up and at 1.00 a.m. on the 18th of October 1981, I surrendered my life to Jesus, as I wholeheartedly welcomed my Lord and Savior Jesus the Son of God into my life. Tears of unspeakable joy flooded me, as I had found my LORD and my GOD. It was and still is the happiest moment of my life when I received Jesus into my life.

I know for sure that my name was immediately inscribed into the Book of Life, as the heavens simultaneously rejoiced with great celebrations as this new soul was ushered into the Kingdom of God.

I had found my first and most precious love – the Lover of my soul is my beloved, and I am His.

I continue to testify that because my salvation is the happiest moment of my life, it follows that my second happiest moment is when another soul is ushered into God's Kingdom.

What happened after that, and how I informed or told my wife Jane, on my return to Malaysia is another story, worthy of a book itself.

Praise the LORD! Hallelujah! Praise the LORD! Hallelujah! Praise the LORD! Hallelujah!

Salvation is so very precious. It is the greatest of all miracles, for even one soul to be saved. The Bible says, "For what profit is it to a man if he gains the whole world and loses his own soul?" [Matthew 16:26 and Mark 8:36]

This means that one precious single soul is worth more in value than the whole world.

Testimony # 057   500 Souls Saved

Since my salvation in 1981, I have been a willing vessel and channel to share the Gospel to others.

For what is more precious than the soul of a person. The word of God says that "What profits a man if he gains the whole world but loses his soul." Matthew 16:26.

We are every ready to recommend others to a good book, a great movie, a fantastic restaurant, a superb holiday site. So, why not tell others, friends relatives and colleagues about the good news, that salvation is from the LORD, and that there is no other name by which we are saved.

Acts 4:12 "Nor is there salvation in any other, for there is no other name under heaven given among men by which we must be saved."

Here and there, now and then, at work and at other times, this vessel, whatever you call me, whether a witness, a disciple of Christ, a fisher of men, an ambassador of Christ, or a little messenger or spokesman, an evangelist or even a lay teacher, preacher or marketplace minister, has been used by the LORD to bring the Good News about Jesus.

Yet, as told in the stories of the "unwilling witness" and the "declaring of a great harvest", it is not me, but just a willing or even an unwilling witness being used by the LORD and the Holy Spirit so that others can come to know and believe in Jesus.

More stories of salvation were related earlier in # 64-68 "My Florist & Plumber Responds, Hard Work Matters, Seed Planting Years, Speedy Harvesting, Set Free from Gangsterism"

Over the years, over 500 souls have now accepted Jesus, through this one vessel or servant, on a personal, and one-to-one basis. Of course, many others may have sowed, and I have just come along to reap, as a coworker or co-laborer for Jesus.

If this vessel can be used to bring that many souls into the Kingdom, what about you? Jesus said that on good soil, "some a hundredfold, some sixty, some thirty" fruits were produced.

Thus, in sharing that I can be used as a channel to bring that many to the Kingdom of God, I am not boasting, but testify that I am just an ordinary vessel like anyone else, and everyone else can do the same, and bring in souls into the Kingdom of God.

Jesus said that "Greater works than this, he (you) will do because I go to My Father."

The only criterion is to 'work hard'; see testimony # 066.

We are good trees, and we can and should bear good fruits. This testimony is extremely important and relevant, as it is the essence and vital principle in my Christian walk and life of nearly forty years.

The best test as Jesus says of a person as too of a tree is in its fruit, and I dare confess, and do so boldly in the name of Jesus Christ, and for the glory of the LORD, and hence the main purpose of the Book, which is not for my name, my fame, or even my gain, truly but that the Name of the LORD be glorified, through the testimonies involving His Son, working through His sons and daughters like me.

For nearly two decades now, I try to live the motto copied from Watchman Nee which says:

"I want nothing for myself; I want everything for my LORD."

In so declaring, do not misunderstand that this author is so righteous and so pure and so good, but that I am merely responding to the truth, or that the truth hits me so deeply and so powerfully that I can have no other motive or motto but that above, because of two verses that govern, rule and guide my life, and are central to my Christian life. These are the two verses below, that proceed forth from the lips of our Lord Jesus.

John 15:5 "For without ME you can do nothing." Or "For apart from Me, you can do nothing."

Luke 18:27 "The things which are impossible with men are possible with God."

The breath that we take in, the oxygen, the water that we drink, the soil or piece of land that we stand on, everything is from Jesus. Hence, John 15:5 is true to the final little atom or speck on earth.

At the end of the day, it is souls that matter, for only the Word of God and souls will remain.

Matthew 24:35 says, "Heaven and earth will pass away, but My words will by no means pass away." John 3:16 declares that we will have eternal life in Jesus.

Thus, leading people to Christ, through the sharing of the Gospel is the key work or labor in our lives.

It is all about souls. Everything else is relatively very much less important.

Testimony # 058 Tongues & Baptism of the Holy Spirit

This is my personal testimony on baptism of the Holy Spirit. It is testimony, not a debate or discussion on the doctrine and interpretation around the Baptism of the Holy Spirit.

At each point in my belief and faith, it is an experience, whether physical, emotional, mental or spiritual.

The first pivotal moment was on the 18th of October 1981 at 1 a.m. in East Birmingham, when I surrendered my life totally to Jesus and I was born again in the Spirit of God as a Christian. Then and there, I wept literally with tears of unspeakable joy, as I was physically, emotionally, mentally and spiritually moved with the knowledge that I had found the Living God, and was confirmed a 'child of God'. I had shifted dramatically from unbelief to believe in the Living God through our Savior Jesus. Simultaneously, the heavens rejoiced that one precious soul was saved.

My second and next important step of faith was when I received my water baptism by full emersion a year after I was saved. This was an important step of faith and a confirmation and a public declaration of my belief as a Christian, in obedience to the Word of God to 'believe and be baptized.'

For me again, this second experience of water baptism was a physical, emotional, mental and spiritual one, one that was filled with joy, peace, assurance and an occasion for celebration.

My third experience being shared here was when I received the baptism of the Holy Spirit and release in tongues which was partly shared in Testimony # 040 "The Photographs".

It was about four years after my salvation when I received the baptism of the Holy Spirit and began to speak in tongues. The desire and search had begun after a sermon I heard at my local pastor at Elim Pentecostal Church in East Finchley, London where I was attending. I continued to seek for this infilling of the Holy Spirit and experienced a relative struggle, requiring a revelation as testified in # 040 "The Photograph".

John the Baptist declared in Matthew 3:11 that Jesus is mightier than he, and He will baptize us with the Holy Spirit and Fire.

In my testimony # 040 "The Photograph", I was prompted by the Holy Spirit to destroy the incriminating photograph and negative showing me bowing before an altar of idols. This was the obstacle hindering me from my being filled with the Holy Spirit and to speak in tongues.

As the Scriptures point out, especially Acts 19:6, "when Paul laid hands on them, the Holy Spirit came upon them, and they spoke with tongues and prophesied." Paul regularly asked the believers whether they had received the Holy Spirit, and when they were filled with the Holy Spirit, the manifestation was the speaking in tongues.

It was around November 1985 when Revered Vincent from Singapore prayed and gave a little push in my belly when I first spoke in tongues. It was a short one then, and I knew that it had happened. It was not as intense an experience as either salvation or water baptism, but I knew that something had happened to me.

It was some years later before I received all kinds of tongues, when a Pastor Ron Sawka from Japan imparted and activated to the congregation "different kinds of tongues".

For me and my personal walk in Christ, this receiving and filling of the Holy Spirit in me led me into the realm of speaking in tongues, singing in the Spirit and the operating of the gifts of the Holy Spirit, one by one.

Is there also a baptism of fire with the release in tongues? I believe so, and the fruits of the ministry is proof of that fire and power. More than 500 souls have been saved through this servant.

Jesus said, "But you shall receive power when the Holy Spirit has come upon you; and you shall be witnesses to Me in Jerusalem, and in all of Judea and Samaria, and to the end of the earth."

I testify that the Holy Spirit dwells in my physical body, as the Word of God says so, and I believe that the Holy Spirit who God our Father has given to us is working through my life to do the things of God, for the extension of God's Kingdom.

I have come to realize the importance of the Holy Spirit in me, in my life, in my being, in my body, which is the Temple of the Holy Spirit, and the Ark of the Covenant.

I welcome and receive the Holy Spirit wholeheartedly as my Counsellor, residing in me, as a part of my thought life, free to speak to me, to guide and teach me, and be my Friend and partner with me in ministry and work for the Kingdom of God.

Is there fire in me? I may not see it, and I may not feel the direct heat, but the Holy Spirit of God in me is FIRE!! I believe it is a spiritual fire, and unseen fire that is seen by spiritual beings and not by human eyes.

Souls saved, many dozens ministered to, miracles and healing seen, the comatose awakened, many were delivered from addiction, from crime, from other sins, and from demonic oppression – these are among the evidence of the fire of God within me, working through this humble servant.

No doubt it did not come in one sudden wave, but it came and continued and is still working through this life, - that is the fire and power of God alive in every believer, when we exercise our faith to serve His Majesty.

Many of the above testimonies are related in this same book, and these testimonies are powerful and true.

What I experience can be no different from any other believer, and any other believer can experience all kinds of gifts, as the Spirit gives, only if we ask, believe and receive in faith.

It is a process that begins when we believe in Jesus, because He said in John 14:12, "Most assuredly, I say to you, he who believes in Me, the works that I do, he will do also; and greater works than these he will do, because I go to My Father."

Testimony # 059   From Coma to Life

Earlier in testimony # 007, a short preaching to a comatose 'beloved' woke her up.

In this testimony, a young lady in her mid-thirties came in to hospital with an "encephalitis' or brain infection or inflammation, caused by a virus, or some other immune process.

It was on a Wednesday night when she came in, under my care as the neurologist on call. The Brain Scan showed a swollen brain, and soon after coming in, she lapsed into coma and had to be ventilated, through Thursday, Friday till Saturday morning.

The rapidity of her illness was frightening, and the brain swelling too. A brain fluid assessment, or Lumbar Puncture should inflammatory cells, pointing more to a viral cause.

I informed the parents the next day that her condition was serious, as she had turned bad so rapidly. We proceeded to give the necessary support and treatment, while she was on a ventilator, including medications to reduce brain swelling.

As they were from a Catholic background, I offered to pray with the parents for her daughter. This was on Thursday late morning, the day after their admission.

She remained stable over Friday, but was still on a ventilator. On Saturday morning, it was the first day and opening of an International Christian Doctors Conference, sponsored and organized by WCDN, or World Christian Doctors' Network, initiated by a church in South Korea. I was a passive attendee.

Right at the beginning, the organizing Chairman, quite unexpectedly asked for any prayer requests especially for healing, and asked for names to be submitted for prayer by an international chain of intercessors, including South Korea.

I immediately thought of Ms Chee and submitted her name for prayer, thinking it was a desperate last resort. I did not think anything further, and continued to attend and was richly blessed by the messages and sermons delivered over the day. I went back to the hospital in the evening, and to my utmost surprise, when I walked into the Intensive Care Unit, where Ms Chee was being ventilated, I saw her sitting up and out of her ventilator.

I asked the nurses, "What happened?"

"Oh, she improved by late morning, and was fighting the endotracheal tube, and the anesthetist decided to extubate her and she has been well since, with her oxygen at 100%"

"That is amazing!" I said, in front of her, and quickly picked up my phone and took a picture of her, sitting up, though looking a little exhausted, being on a ventilator and endotracheal tube for the past 2 ½ days.

I immediately recalled that we had put her name for prayer. I told Ms Chee that, and said that the whole conference and churches linked to Korea were praying for her.

I told my nurses, mostly Muslim, that it was a miracle. "Ini betulnya mukjizat." They too, had been equally amazed at her rapid turnaround.

The fact that it was a supernatural miracle was confirmed the next morning, when Jesus appeared at her bedside, smiling at her, during a short visit.

It was a Sunday, and I was at the conference. On my return, she excitedly told me that afternoon that, "Jesus visited her, and smiled at her", before vanishing.

"Wow, amazing, and what did Jesus say?" I asked.

"He just smiled at me."

I took out my handphone, and took a video recording, asking her the same questions.

This testimony was presented at the next WCDN International Conference in Valencia, Spain, and everyone was blessed by this awesome testimony.

A critically ill comatose patient, with severe brain swelling from an "encephalitis" was ventilated for nearly three days, when she suddenly became better and could breathe on her own. From late Wednesday night to Saturday morning, she was ill and on a ventilator. By late Saturday, morning, she was out of a ventilator, and sitting up.

That coincided with the prayer period for the sick with her name listed among those who needed prayers.

Jesus came the next morning to confirm that He was the Healer who turned the illness around.

Ms Chee, like all the people whom I know who have seen Jesus, each and every one of them, know almost instantly that Jesus is Jesus, when they see Him.

How is my faith strengthened by this testimony?

The LORD is real, and for the most of us, we do not need to see Him to believe in Him; yet the LORD does appear to His people from time to time.

Testimony # 060   Jesus appears to my Cousin

Seeing the Lord Jesus is a special and precious experience. Quite a few people I know have seen or met the Lord Jesus. Some of my own encounters either in dreams, or with Him being seen beside me are related in this book. This particular story is related by my cousin.

My cousin is a relatively sensitive person with spiritual eyes, enabling him to see the spirit realm. There were times, he related to me what he saw around us, when we were visiting a friend's house, or along the road that we were passing by.

He, like me comes from a Buddhist Taoist background and he would relate to me the incidents he experienced especially during the so-called Chinese ghost month.

I shared the Good News to him, and he did follow me to church on a couple of occasions. He described how there were angels during the church service, and he saw two angels hovering over the pulpit as my resident Pastor Chew was preaching.

One visit to church was not enough for him to believe until his own personal experience of visitations from the Lord Jesus. Jesus visited him three times, and I will relate just two of those visits.

The first visit occurred while he was about to sleep, when Jesus suddenly appeared at the foot of his bed. He immediately cried out to him, "Jesus, Jesus", as his spirit immediately knew the Lordship of Jesus, and His Presence.

He told me that they communicated by telepathic transfer, as no audible words were spoken. He grieved and cried for help, as he had been without a job for over ten years since, depending on his siblings for sustenance.

The conversation went on for about twenty minutes. At the end my cousin embraced the Lord

Jesus, weeping with joy. Jesus then went on to tell my cousin this:

"Go and see your cousin," refereeing to me, and he did exactly that the next day. I took him out shopping and paid for his groceries, and sent him home. I did help him on and off, and he managed to survive with assistance from his sisters.

The second visit to the same cousin took place on another night when Jesus appeared beside him, standing on my cousin's side. He was immediately filled with joy and excitement.

Suddenly, on the other side was none other the adversary. He described him so vividly that it tallied with all the pictures that has been drawn in comics to depict the adversary of the Truth. also, at his womb. He had red blood shot eyes, with horns on his scalp, and his skin was rough and scaly, and nails were sharp like claws, and he had a tail.

He came by on the left and urged my cousin, with persuasive words, saying, "Follow me, follow me."

My cousin felt fear and immediately declared, "No, I will follow Jesus." At the mention of Jesus, the adversary vanished. The vision ended then and there.

Altogether, Jesus appeared to my cousin three times, and seeing the Lord in person secured his belief and place in eternity. His woes did not end, as he unfortunately suffered a stroke, and is now staying in a nursing home.

What a privilege to have seen and met Jesus three times by then!

Many people have sensitive eyes and can see the spiritual realm, but seeing our Savior Jesus is special. Skeptics may scoff at it, but for those who have seen Jesus, they know immediately that it is Him, and the adversary cannot and dare not pretend to be Jesus.

Many will casually say that unless they see Jesus, they would not believe. One thing that is consistent for all who have seen Him, and that is, when they see Jesus, each one immediately knows that it is Him. There are countless testimonies on the internet about people who have seen Jesus.

Our Lord Jesus is real and the Son of God; even though we generally do not see Him, yet He is actually by our side. [Psalm 16:8]. He has been appearing to many people over the past 2000 years since His resurrection and ascension. The Bible says that the pure in heart will see God.

That is the Truth that when we seek the Truth, we will find Him, whether by sight (uncommon), by knowing (very common, if not always), by feeling (quite often) and by faith, always.

This author is also struck by the reality of this testimony that the 'adversary of mankind' was described as how the comic books show Him, and that with the mention of our Majesty's Name, - Jesus, the King of kings, he fled.

James 4:7 says, "Therefore submit to God, resist the devil and he will flee from you."

And since we are just there, we are reminded of James 4:8, which says, "Draw near to God and He will draw near to you."

Testimony # 061   Instant Healing & Visitation During Prayer

This is such an awesome testimony told to me by my patient that it should be retold and retold again and again.

It is one of those dramatic instances of healing, deliverance, and salvation taking place all in one prayer, with a visitation by Jesus simultaneously.

She was a Chinese lady in her late fifties. She related to me this amazing testimony that happened in Kuala Lumpur.

She had gone to China for a short trip with her husband. Unfortunately, soon after that visit, on her return, she had developed an inflammation of the brain which was diagnosed as an "encephalitis". During that short illness, she was drowsy, confused and had lost her memory. The trip to China, - all of it was wiped out from her memory even until today.

Due to her illness and in desperation, despite her being a Taoist/Buddhist at that time, someone brought her to church for prayers.

She described what happened below.

"I remember being prayed for. I was seated down in a chair, when the pastor prayed for me. He placed his hand on my head and began to pray. Immediately, I saw Jesus several feet in front of me. He was bright, shining and golden. I was overwhelmed with joy and love, and started weeping profusely, as I called out to His Name, "Jesus, Jesus". I recognized and knew Him at once, and it was like I had known Him for a long time, and that I was meeting an old good friend. Simultaneously, as I cried out to Jesus, I could feel and see hundreds of needles flying off from my whole body, from the head, body and limbs. I was also instantly healed, and my mind, conscious self fully restored instantly."

Her husband was with her; the whole family i.e. she, husband, and children all accepted Jesus as their God and Savior, and stopped worshipping idols.

Hearing such an awesome testimony has edified me, encouraged me and truly strengthened my spirit man, for that is what I would have considered the perfect prayer when we pray for the sick. I have been praying for the sick for four decades, and this is the most powerful testimony of an instant prayer, where healing, deliverance and salvation to the whole family, with the glorious privilege of seeing Jesus occurring in one single instance!

Hallelujah, praise the LORD!
Hallelujah, praise the LORD!
Hallelujah, praise the LORD!

Naturally, I was very keen to look for the church and the man of God whose prayers turned out to be the perfect prayer. As God intended, the church and man of God remains unknown and a mystery to me. I realize subsequently, that it is not the church or the person, but the LORD that matters.

This 'perfect prayer' can take place anywhere by anyone, and it is probably happening all the time, with every prayer when the Name of the Lord is being evoked, only if we believe.

May this testimony inspire every believer to pray, believing in the Name of Jesus, and all things will be possible with God.

What did I receive from this testimony?

A prayer in the Name of Jesus can do wondrous healing, deliverance and salvation, with the Lord's visitation; let us continue to pray without ceasing in all situations.

Testimony # 062   The Cross Spoke to Him

This yet another awesome and powerful testimony that happened at work, in a normal day. This is the marketplace ministry that can happen to you and I, if only we believe and exercise our faith by doing works for God.

This patient, a Malaysian Chinese was in his early forties. He had been admitted to hospital for a heart attack and a stroke, both at the same time. He was in the Coronary Care Unit, and it was about a week after his admission, when I saw him. I was not his doctor, but as his doctor was on leave for a few days, I was a covering or 'replacement' doctor taking the primary doctor's job.

He was married with a Malaysian wife and child, but was having an adulterous relationship with a Chinese national. There he was in the hospital bed, subdued with a blank stare and not talking for over a week. His vital signs i.e. blood pressure, pulse, oxygenation, respiration rate were all stable, and he was breathing on his own with nasal oxygen. I noted some tattoo marks on his left arm, and his hair was dyed in bright brownish color.

Something was not right about him, though. Normally, with what he had, he should be able to talk, and respond. The nurses also felt so, that it was odd that he was not awake or talking, since his vital signs were stable.

I soon found out that he was a Christian. A thought came into my mind – a Godly idea. I saw a couple of plastic straws by the bedside. They were red in color. This happened before single use plastic straws were discouraged, though still not banned.

I picked up two straws and made a cross with it, a red one too and showed it to him, asking him in sign language to pray, by showing the next sign of my two clasped hands. I urged him to pray and to call upon the Name of Jesus. I did this a few times for two days in a row.

On the third day, he started talking. This is his testimony.

He said, "When I entered this hospital, on the first day, satan visited me seventy times. He also sent me messages (SMS and texts) on my phone. I was terrified, afraid, and totally devastated."

One can guess the sort of messages and the purpose of those visits. It was when he saw me, and followed my urging to pray to Jesus that hope returned, and fear left.

He began to improve day by day and was discharged within a few days.

A month later, amazingly I saw him running on the treadmill in the physiotherapy department. I greeted him, and he responded by saying, "Thank you Jesus! Jesus healed me!"

I took out my handphone and asked him to repeat it, and recorded him running at moderate pace on the treadmill saying, "Thank you Jesus!"

What an awesome testimony! He was deceived to believe that he had no hope, by not just one visit but seventy visits followed by messages from the same adversary of mankind, until one humble servant came along. And it was his own prayers that nullified all the plans of the enemy.

The Name of the Lord Jesus is powerful and when we call upon His Name in prayer, there is healing, deliverance and salvation into the Heavenly Kingdom.

What did I learn from this testimony?

The adversary is always around to wreck. Be wary of the one who steals, kills and destroys, and he is a liar. Trust always in the Lord Jesus, our Friend and Savior. Jesus speaks the Truth. He is our protector, defender, helper and God.

Testimony # 063   From Atheist to Believer

Philip (not his real name) entered my office in a wheelchair, pushed by his lovely wife. He was a senior lawyer, who during his time, according to his son, could out-argue anyone. He was such a learned man, a man whose mind ticks probably faster than the clock, one among a few brothers of accomplished lawyers.

This happened over two decades ago, when I was still in public service as a consultation neurologist. The door of my government clinic practice then was about twelve feet from my consultation chair. I could see his condition as soon as he entered the room. It was the first time we met. His wife gave a warm smile, while he was clearly down and depressed. Strokes paralyze one's face, and at best, a smile becomes a frown or even a scowl. It was obvious that he was a victim of devastating strokes, bringing down a man of great stature into this humbled state. I immediately had a deep sense of compassion on him, and when he was about four feet and still being pushed towards my table, I called out to him and said this, below.

"Hi, good morning Philip. Can I pray for you?"

Here was I, a doctor and stranger to him, having just met him about 3-5 seconds only, offering to pray for him. I had seen the name 'Philip' and assumed that he was a believer in Jesus Christ, and compassion had filled me. It was the most natural thing for me to do, as a believer and a humble 'marketplace worker' for the Lord. Little did I know, as his wife would tell me later, than this learned man raised as an Anglican church goer, would become a professing atheist in his later adult years.

Almost immediately, he yelled and verbally lashed back at me, with a slurred but louder than audible voice, probably mustered from the depths of his soul.

"No! I don't want! Don't touch me! Don't pray for me!!"

I was stunned for two seconds, as it was a very firm and clear rejection of my offer to pray for him. I stayed calm, gave him a warm smile, and spoke in a gentle, though non-apologetic tone.

"It's okay, Philip, I won't pray for you now, but I will pray for you in my own quiet time."

He was silent. As a learned man, he must have understood that I was not giving up, and that I would still pray for him in my own private and quiet time.

I told him and his wife quite frankly that I was on a forty-day fast, and there were four people in particular on my prayer list, and I would add him as the fifth.

He made no comment or response to my statements, and we proceeded with the neurological consultation, which lasted perhaps around half an hour, and we parted in a friendly tone. Neither apologized to each other, as there was no need. Again, a learned man understands and often with that understanding there is no need to say anything further.

That is why the scriptures says in Proverbs 17:10, "Rebuke is more effective for a wise man than a hundred blows to a fool."

About three months later, Philip came back for review. Again, at the door, with the wife pushing the wheel chair, we made eye contact but with a significant difference.

Tania, his wife gave a warm and big smile and declared positively:

"Doc, Philip is now born again!"

"Wow! Really Philip?" I exclaimed, as both of us were filled with emotions. He nodded with confirmation from a distance. A wonderful feeling of joy and excitement filled my inner being. Here was a man, a self-professed atheist, who had been very critical and antagonistic to the Christian faith for decades but has now just been born again.

As he came nearer on the same wheelchair, as I asked lovingly: "Can I pray for you?"

Tears flowed and streamed down both cheeks, as he nodded in acceptance.

We prayed, and his wife related to me that finally after 25 years of longsuffering and being persecuted by him, Philip had finally come to believe in Jesus.

The following week, I visited him in his house. He welcomed me and again agreed to prayers; we prayed the sinner's prayers together as we welcomed Jesus again, as our Lord and Savior.

Cynics or skeptics may doubt, but here was a man who was dead against the faith on one visit, and turned around in the next. This humble servant does not claim full credit or any credit at all, but was privileged to be one of the final cogs that turned the wheels of unbelief to belief, being used as a for the Holy Spirit to do work for the Kingdom of God.

Our God, the LORD answers prayers. Among the five whom I was fasting and praying for, fast forward to now, four have responded and accepted the LORD and gone home to the Heavenly abode. The fifth is still around.

What have I learned from this testimony?

Don't give up on your stubborn loved ones or friends. And the LORD is not slow or slack but is patient and desires that all come to repentance and none perish. [2 Peter 3:9] Jesus

came to set the captives free - physical, mental, emotional, spiritual captives.

Salvation is just around the corner.

Testimony # 064   God's Sound Shield

This is yet another awesome testimony of God being at work with me, helping me along at critical moments, when I needed His help.

Mr. Chan (not his real name) was senior Malaysian Chinese businessman recently retired from the insurance industry. He had seen me once or twice before, and had come to the emergency department in a private hospital where I was a practicing neurologist. His son, a believer had accompanied him.

I knew that he was not yet a believer in Jesus, and I had previously wanted to share the Gospel to him, but did not have the opportunity. I somehow felt the urgency to share to him this time around. I had to do it.

However, there were two 'obstacles', - one being that it was an open area, in the emergency bay, where two to four patients were located. The other was that he was hard of hearing. It was also timely that he was accompanied by his son, who was a believer, as other family members were not. It was my experience that the presence of another non-believer made it very difficult if not awkward for the sharing of the 'Good News'.

I approached and greeted Mr. Chan, and without hesitation. Since I had felt the prompting of the Holy Spirit, I proceeded to share to him about Jesus, with the intention of leading him to salvation on that day. Amazingly, the moment I opened my mouth to share about Jesus, and I had to speak loudly as he was hard of hearing, I saw and heard "God's Sound Shield" operating instantly.

"Mr. Chan, I want to urge you to receive Jesus as your Lord and Savior…", was how I had begun, and simultaneously when I said, "Mr. Chan…", a five year old girl three feet away, on the next bed from us started yelling and screaming on top of her voice, as the medical officer had begun to set an intravenous line and drip for her.

I have always felt that a separate emergency ward should be set up for children as they will cry, yell and scream when they are unwell or when any painful procedure was being done on them.

Here was just another situation. I was too busy on my own sharing the Gospel, shouting quite loudly thankful that the LORD had given me a "Shield of Sound" so that what I said was not heard by others around me.

Mr. Chan responded to my sharing and agreed to receive Jesus as his Lord and Savior, and then and there he followed me, phrase by phrase, saying the sinner's prayer as follows.

"Father God, I believe in your Son, Jesus Christ who died for all our sins, and is the Savior of the World. I receive you Lord Jesus, as my Lord and Savior. Come into my life, and forgive me of all my sins. I am now a child of God, born by the Spirit of Christ. Thank you, LORD. I pray all these in Jesus' Mighty Name. Amen."

Exactly on the dot, at the very moment we said 'amen', the child stopped crying. The precise timing of the child's screaming and crying had begun when I said, "Mr. Chan", and had perfectly ended when we said 'amen' was to me definitely God's Hand.

Our Father is so perfect in His Timing, and ushering of Mr. Chan into the Heavenly Kingdom, providing for us a shield or wall that gave us sound-proofing, all within barely three to four feet away. I was truly very excited that Mr. Chan had come to know Jesus, and was indeed hoping a man of his influence could touch other men and women and lead them to Christ Jesus.

God's ways are definitely higher than ours, for within barely two weeks, he suddenly went home to be with Jesus. On reflecting back, I now understand the urgency of his calling upon the Name of Jesus, for he was barely a 'baby' of two weeks of age in Christ, when he was called home. I am moved that I was obedient to the Holy Spirit to share at that critical time that gave him the passport into Heaven.

What have I learned from this testimony?

When we step out in faith, trusting in The LORD and believing in Him, He is there with us without fail.

There are lost ones out there that need someone to speak to them about Jesus. Anybody can do it; somebody should do it; everybody thinks somebody will do it, but sometimes nobody did it. Am I or you that somebody to stand in the gap for that lost soul?

Testimony # 065   Seed Planting Years

We often long for instant results and immediate answers to prayers, like the lady with the perfect prayer, # Testimony 061, where everything happened and she was healed, delivered and saved in one go. However, often there is a process of sowing, praying, waiting, before one can reap and rejoice when salvation happens.

This testimony is about God's faithfulness, and trusting Him, while we faithfully sow seeds of faith, and wait for God's timing.

I was posted to Sarawak from 1982-1987. During that period when I was a young Christian, being just saved in 1981 and growing in the Word of God, having just been baptized by full emersion (1982), and also the Baptism of the Holy Spirit (1985), I was on fire for the LORD.

I recall inviting friends and colleagues to evangelistic meetings. For one particular meeting, an American evangelist held meetings for a few nights. I invited close to fifty people for the particular meeting, and seventeen of them came, including my eldest brother who happened to be visiting Kuching.

I sat at the back of the hall, and waited patiently for the closing and altar call, where the audience were invited to receive Jesus as their Lord and Savior.

When the meeting ended, I counted among my invited guests that not a single one had responded. In other words, it seemed like my efforts had produced `zero' results.

This did not discourage me, as I continued to share the Good News. My joy and celebration came in much later, when among those who had heard the 'Good News', some five to eight years later, - one by one had called me to say, "Doc, I am now born again!"

I recall also how I used to share with one elderly gentleman in his mid-seventies, and there was no clear response, often just a polite smile.

Some years later, when I visited Kuching, he was ill and in a semi-comatose state. He was still able to recognize my voice and acknowledge me with eyes closed. I urged him to call upon Jesus as Lord and Savior. As, he held my hand, I urged him to squeeze it in response if he agreed to call upon the Name of Jesus. He willingly squeezed my fingers a couple of times as an agreement to call upon the Name of the Lord.

This testimony is about sowing and planting seeds, and keeping at it, without waiting for a response. We can trust that the seed has been planted and that the LORD will work on the individual and bring Him to salvation.

One of my words of persuasion or parting words is this: "If ever you are in trouble, or whenever you are in danger and in need of help, just call upon Jesus, - call upon the Name of Jesus, and He will help you."

What have I learned from these experiences?

Like the farmer, we may not see immediate results or response. We must sow and wait, and trust and believe that the Word has gone forth and will not return void.

Isaiah 55:11 "So shall My word be that goes forth from My mouth; it shall not return to Me void."

Testimony # 066   Hard Work Matters

While this book is about awesome testimonies and miracles, this particular testimony relates to sheer human effort.

Jesus said clearly, and it applies to us too in John 9:4, "I must work the works of Him who sent Me while it is day; night is coming when no one can work."

Again, in Luke 10:2, Jesus said, "The harvest truly is great, but the laborers are few; therefore, pray the Lord of the harvest to send out laborers into His harvest."

This is my testimony of "hard work" and how it matters.

It was in 1991, when I was about ten years in the faith. I was transferred from my wife's hometown of Kuala Terengganu to Kuala Lumpur, the capital city of Malaysia. It was a major move, the second after my qualification as a specialist. The first four or five years was spent in Kuching, at a time of my early spiritual growth. The atmosphere there in Sarawak was positive very enriching for me as a young Christian.

The next four years in Kuala Terengganu was very different, literally dry if not extremely restricted for a believer. Kuala Lumpur in contrast is bustling, full of activity and with plenty of resources and opportunity for everything.

As I was alone in the city for a few initial months, before the rest of the family came over, I enrolled myself in a "Deeper Life Seminar" conducted by Reverend Vernon and Margareth Falls. There was a series of night meetings conducted over a full month.

During the period of the seminar, we were asked to set our own targets, with respect to how many souls to be saved through our personal effort over that period. I was ambitious and set a number of thirty souls to be saved in that one month.

Little did I know that it was to be an exercise and training for the rest of my Christian walk that taught me this vital lesson that "hard work matters."

I worked very hard each day, after work to reach out for the unsaved. When we pray for opportunities and openings, God will open doors. George Whitefield's prayer was: "Give me souls or I die." Mine was less emphatic but it was my sincere target to win a soul a day for that period of a month.

The seminar and the month completed and I did a tally. I fell short of my target of "30 souls", as I had led 'only ten' to Christ in that period. It was still a good effort to bring ten souls to the

Kingdom of God. The revelation I had from this exercise struck a deep chord in my heart.

Suddenly my eyes opened to the fact that "hard work matters.'

I realized that over the past ten years as a Christian, half of which was spent in Sarawak, and the other half in Terengganu, with two years in the United Kingdom, I was instrumental in leading only ten souls into the Kingdom of God. Yet, in this one month of dedicated, committed hard work, the same number of ten souls got saved! The first ten years brought in ten souls, and now ten souls were ushered in, in just one month, all through sheer hard work.

Therefore, we need to labor for the LORD, and hard work will bring in the fruits of our labor, in multiples of ten, sixty or a hundred-fold.

Sowing has to come before reaping, and when we sow in tears (which include prayers from the heart), we will reap with joy. (Psalm 126:5)

What have I learned over the years?

There is therefore no short cut to bearing fruit. Hard work matters. Any worker, farmer, fisherman or gardener knows that hard work bears fruit.

Testimony # 067   My Florist & Plumber Responds

This testimony of my florist and plumber is about people whom we have known for a long time, and whom we have yet to share the Good News with.

It was the first of January a few years ago, when I found myself in the market with my wife. I was restless as I wanted to be in church for the first service of the year, and was delayed. I expressed my frustration that I was not in church, and told the LORD, "LORD, lead me to someone to share the Good News."

I walked a short distance in the market and saw my florist, Jenny (not her real name) and decided to talk to her. I have known Jenny for over a dozen years, as she was working as a dental assistant before.

I went directly to her and spoke this first sentence, "Good morning Jenny, and Happy New Year. I want to share with you about Jesus."

Her immediate response was, "Oh, I want to be a Christian, but I do not how?"

I was truly shocked if not ashamed of myself, that all through these years, passing by her almost weekly, I had not stopped to share the Good News to her. She had been keen to know more about the Christian faith, and she had also wanted to be a Christian, but did not know how!

Over the next few minutes, I shared about Jesus to her, and led her to the sinner's prayers. She then asked me what to do with her little statues and idols. I advised her that we will arrange for her to join a cell group, and they will take her through that process.

A few weeks after that situation, I was all fired up to share with people around me. Now, it was my plumber.

My plumber had come over to fix a few things around my house. It was quite a busy afternoon for him, requiring at least about two hours of work. While he was going around fixing the plumbing, I was preparing to share with him. I said in my heart clearly that this is the day that I would share with him. I had known him for nearly twenty years, and he had been a responsible, reliable and trusted plumber.

I prepared tea and biscuits, and when he had finished, I invited him to sit down.

This is not a common thing for a plumber to be treated with tea and biscuits, as most plumbers after doing their jobs tend to be not so clean, and would hardly feel comfortable to sit down for tea with the owner.

I insisted, and he must have felt uncomfortable, when I said, "Please sit down."

I proceeded directly and told him that I would like to share about Jesus to him.

His immediate response was, "Oh, my mother is a Christian."

"What?" I said, partly stunned and surprised. "What about you, then?" I asked.

"Oh, in my family, as for religion, the boys followed the father, while the girls follow the mother", was his reply.

I then said, "I feel that it is a good thing if you give your life to Jesus. He is the Savior of the world."

Mr. Lai (not his real name), the plumber conceded, said a simple prayer and gave his life to Jesus, on that day.

What have I learned from these two episodes?

There are many people around us, who are ready and willing to accept Jesus. They need a nudge, a little tug, or a little push, to make that critical decision, and we should be that

ambassador, that fisher of men, who should lead them gently into the Kingdom of God.

Testimony # 068   Speedy Harvesting

Apart from the two stories above, with my plumber and florist, people who are known to me and ones who are ready to receive Jesus, here are a few stories with strangers, who very quickly too are ushered into the Kingdom of God.

Jesus said that the harvest is plentiful and laborers are few.

I was referred a middle-aged man who was suffering from AIDS, or advanced HIV infection. This was in the early nineties, when a diagnosis of AIDS meant death in three years, as there was no cure then.

I picked up his notes, and was walking towards his bed, some fifteen feet away, when compassion engulfed me, and I directly raised the question, as my first sentence to him.

I said, "Mr. Pang, you have a serious illness. Why don't you give your life to Jesus?"

He looked at me and responded, "OK, doctor." We said the sinner's prayers together, and after that only, did I proceed to assess him. I asked him why he was so open to receive Jesus, and he replied that one of his relatives was a Christian.

While we were conversing, the neighboring patient, also a Chinese overheard and was observing us. I turned around to face him, and asked him the same question, "What about you, Sir?"

His reply surprised me, for he said, "I am a Christian too, but I have backslided."

I then said, "Then, come back to Jesus." He will bless you.

Two persons were touched and ministered to in one instance.

On another occasion, in my clinic, a young male Indonesian Chinese came for a consultation. I was led to share with him about Jesus. He responded affirmatively and welcomed Jesus into his life.

After the prayer, I asked him why he had so easily accepted Jesus.

He said, "Doc, I saw Jesus standing behind you."

"Oh, praise the LORD. I have never seen Him, but I know that He is beside me."

It was my last night at the Deeper Life Seminar series. I had set a target of 30 souls to be won for Jesus, over that one month. I dropped by to see a cousin. He was the fourth of siblings who still had not given his life to Jesus, when both parents and all his siblings had made that commitment. I figured out it would be fast and easy.

I pressed the bell and at the gate, while he was just at the door, I called out to him,

"Arnold (not his real name), tonight, you should give your life to Jesus!"

He gave a short laugh and said "Okay". He said the sinner's prayer and then I left. He has had enough told to him and has witnessed enough to know about the truth in Jesus. I assumed that his siblings would follow up with him. I met him again recently and encouraged him to start an active church life. This is 20 years on. He said, "OK."

Everyone's walk is different. Like what Reinhart Bonke said, there is an A to Z in one's walk, and he does the "A" or conversion in leading them to Christ, and there are others who continue with the discipleship.

I feel the same too. Though I do not follow-up all of them, on and off, I will meet some who will remind me that I was the one who led them, their parents or their loved ones to Christ.

What do I learn from these testimonies?

We should seek out the lost and look for opportunities to share Christ and His love, and as St Francis Assisi said, speak if necessary.

We can persuade, but it is never for us to pressure and push. Our role is to share and tell them about Jesus. It is the Holy Spirit who will do the conviction. The seed is sowed, and some immediately respond, but some will do so at a later date.

Testimony # 069   Set Free from Gangsterism

Lau San (not his real name) walked into my clinic, together with three men, his honchos, as I would find out later. He demanded to be seen, as he was suffering from headaches. It was the lunch hour, and I usually use that hour to review patients that are already admitted in the wards. I did not know he was, so I told him to wait till I get back at 2 p.m. He waited patiently till I returned.

I came back on time at 2 p.m., and proceeded to see him. By that time, I had guessed that he had links to the underworld. In fact, he controlled a small township.

I told him that he must be a big brother or "Taiko", similar to that of a Mafia boss locally. He said, "Yes, in Rawang."

He then told me that he had been on the death row twice, almost scheduled to be hung to death, but somehow was able to get out free.

It was at this point that I told him that it was time to stop and to give his life to Jesus. He looked at me, and within a short while agreed. I called his honchos in, and I spoke to all four of them about Jesus, and who Jesus was.

All four of them gave their lives to Jesus. I picked up my phone and called for help from Ps Jason and my good friend and evangelist Brother Tek Seng. They came and ministered to all four of them. The lead gangster, who had come to see me, led another ten or eleven of his men to Jesus.

A few weeks later, he came back and affirmed that they have left dark world activities, and now confessed that it was "tough to earn a living." I told him to trust in the LORD and He will see him through the difficult times.

What have I learned from this episode?

There is no one too evil or too great a sinner to be beyond redemption. Even those in criminal activities have a conscience, and when touched by the Spirit of God, they are born again. It is no wonder that many, many people in detention or prison come to know Jesus as their Savior.

Testimony # 070   Post Tsunami Harvest

Following on the lesson about "hard work does matter", I seized the opportunity in January 2005.

Living in Malaysia, we were next door to the devastating tsunami, and the northern part of Malaysia was affected, with some dozens of lives lost. The city of Penang saw even fishing boats washed on to the city streets, though what happened in my country was minimal compared to Sumatra and Thailand, where thousands upon thousands perished.

An estimated 230,000 people perished over a few hours, and three testimonies # 28-30 are related earlier.

The sense of the preciousness of life, and the suddenness of death was in the air. The tsunami, which is perhaps the most devastating in the history of mankind in recent years, had happened on Boxing Day, a day after Christmas.

I told and pledged to the LORD that I would work hard for souls for the month of January, which would begin barely five days after the tragedy.

Thus, from January 1st to January 31st 2005, I worked very hard at almost every opportunity, and recorded each salvation by name, with phone contact. In my testimony on "Hard Work Matters" i.e. testimony # 67, a total number of 10 souls were won for the Kingdom of God.

For that month of January 2005, when the whole world mourned for over 200,000 souls who perished suddenly, a total of 63 souls were saved. That is the greatest harvest of souls on a personal basis in one month. I have not been able to repeat it, probably because I have not work as hard at that month since.

When even one soul is saved, the Heavens rejoice. I am overjoyed that a good number of people came to know Jesus through me for the month after the tsunami. All Glory goes to our LORD for His mercy and compassion.

What have I learned from this testimony?

The harvest is plentiful and laborers are few. The Holy Spirit will work alongside us in convicting these lost souls.

Testimony # 071   The Horizon – God shows a sign

I have never seen a vision from God so far. This short testimony is about signs in the sky, two so far that I have seen from the LORD. I will relate one on 'The Horizon'.

I was in Indonesia in Jakarta and staying at a hotel called `Hotel Horison' for a couple of days. This particular hotel was named after the horizon, as it is situated right on the equator, though there is a chain of hotels by that name.

I was very tired the first night I checked in, and for that reason I woke up late, as late as 9 a.m. on that first morning. The sun was shining brightly along the bay that morning. I could see the sea shore, with the sun beaming brightly on my far-right corner, appearing just between two tall buildings.

I then heard a still small voice, "Watch the horizon. Watch the horizon."

I recognized that it was the Holy Spirit telling me. So, I replied, "Okay, but the sun has risen."

I then took it to mean that I was to watch the sun rise over the horizon the next morning.

For the next morning, I set the alarm clock as early as 5.30 a.m. as when I checked with the hotel reception, I was told that the sun rises as early as 6 a.m. in the morning. In Malaysia, because of the time adjustment, the sun rises at about 7 a.m.

I got up punctually, at 5.30 a.m., being obedient to the Spirit of God and headed for the beach and waited for the sun to rise. It was dark, but there were people around at that time.

I then saw four pictures, around the rising of the sun, as the Holy Spirit of God spoke to me, and interpreted the sign I saw over the horizon.

The first picture was on of sheer darkness over the ocean.

The next view or sight that appeared was a very broad glimmer of light appearing across the ocean right in front of me, over the horizon, the glimmer being cast throughout the middle of the sea in front of me. My first thought was, "is this where the sun is about to rise?" I kept my gaze fixed on the sea in the direction of the glimmer. I had at that moment forgotten what I had seen the morning before. This glimmer lasted perhaps about ten minutes or more.

Then came the third picture. Suddenly, the sun appeared on the far right, and I recalled where I had seen it the morning before. It was bright red, and oddly, it cast a very small and narrow reflection over the sea. Nevertheless, there was no doubt at all, that this is the sun, the true sun that rises up without fail for the earth every day. By then, the broad glimmer of light over the horizon had disappeared.

This third view lasted barely a few minutes, with its bright reflection and then the sun disappeared under the clouds, and it was bright morning.

The Holy Spirit gave me the full interpretation then and there.

The first view before the sun came up: "The World is in DARKNESS"

The second view, a broad glimmer: "This is the wide and FALSE PATH". It does not lead to the Son.

The third view, the narrow reflection: "This is the TRUE LIGHT of the World." He came briefly to show Himself to the world.

The fourth view, as the sun disappears into the clouds: "This is the PRESENT-DAY World." They do not know the Son, and do not know what is the right path now that the Son has appear and risen up.

"This is the true sun (Son), and the path (reflections) is narrow, while the broad bright path (a deception) is the wrong path of the world. The true sun (Son) appeared for a moment for you to see, and then vanished under the clouds."

I believe this phenomenon is not new, and probably can be seen with most sun rises, that the sea and ocean brighten up as a bright beaming light from the horizon, and the real sun may appear to its left or right, and not necessarily from the direction where the initial beaming light comes from.

What did I learn from this testimony?

God does show us signs sometimes in the skies, and it is the Spirit's prompting that makes those signs meaningful, when we receive the correction interpretation.

The sign was shown to me and I experienced it myself. God can give you a sign for you to too, if you so desire.

Testimony # 072   Elderlies Saved after Two Decades of Prayers

One of the greatest concerns, burdens and worries, even though we should never worry as a Christian is the salvation of our loved ones.

In that respect, I am so thankful to my LORD, and also forever thankful for a faithful servant who stood in the gap for my dad. I came to know the LORD in 1981, and was the first in my immediate family. My dad came to Christ in 1984, thanks to a faithful aunty, Madam Khoo Siew Gaik, who has since gone on too to be with the LORD. As for my dad, I did two things. One was to tell him in 1981 that I had become a Christian. He gave me his blessings. On another occasion, I gave him a Bible as a gift. I did not share the Gospel to him, out of respect and honor, just in case he said something negative.

Aunty Khoo as I called her, invited my dad to a few Christian meetings. It was in one rally in a stadium by Scott McKinney in Kuala Lumpur that he gave his life to Jesus and never looked back. He was subsequently a changed man, full of joy and always talking about Jesus. For the record, it was Aunty Khoo who also inspired me to keep on winning souls for God. At my last encounter with her, after wholeheartedly thanking her for helping to lead my dad to Jesus, I asked her how many souls she has won for God. The answer was "400." For that reason, I started counting and set my own target to exceed that number, to emulate Aunty Khoo though not to compete with her.

This testimony, partly told in # 13 "The Unwilling Witness", is about an elderly couple, both in the mid-eighties. Tam & Tay (not their real names) were marketplace professionals serving in Beijing. They had been there for about two decades, with two unsaved elderlies back home in Malaysia. They had naturally been praying for his parents for that period, believing, trusting and knowing that these two would be saved one day. They just did not know when or how.

With elderly unsaved parents in the Malaysian Chinese or Indian context, there are several issues and obstacles, among which is language, culture and practices, apart from the original religious beliefs. It is difficult for the children to persuade the parents, as the common reply is that "they have eaten more salt than we have eaten rice", and that they should follow the faith of their forefathers.

Thus, when these two were unwell, Tam & Tay accompanied them to see me. They saw a Scripture verse on the wall on the "Fruit of the Spirit", and Tay, the daughter-in-law interrupted me half-way through my medical examination and asked me to share the Gospel to her father-in-law.

It had happened on a day, when I was not willing and the LORD was about to show His Mighty Hand. As I had related in that testimony # 013 "The Unwilling Witness", the elderly couple gave their lives to Jesus, one after the other.

It may have taken twenty years, but it is better late than never. Some are ushered in very fast; some take ages, years and years, perhaps even after you and I have gone. It is not for us to ask why, to be upset, but only to trust, for God is never slow or slack.

2 Peter 3:9 "The LORD is not slack (or slow) concerning His promise, as some count slackness, but is longsuffering toward us, not willing that any should perish, but that all should come to repentance."

Don't give up on your loved ones!

What have I learned from his testimony?

Don't give up on your loved ones! They will be saved, you and your household. This author is still waiting patiently for his beloved Jane to be saved, now 38 years of waiting.

Testimony # 073   Grandpa Finally Saved

I continue with another grandfather story.

A man in his early fifties was admitted under my care for a stroke. The stroke was mild, but nevertheless required admission.

On the third day, I noticed that he had a big Bible by his bed side. I am a collector of Bibles, and currently have over a dozen of different versions and sizes, but have never seen one so big. These are the Bibles which are placed at the altars in churches, perhaps purchased only by special order.

It was in the Mandarin version.

"Wow!" I said, "You must be someone prominent in the church!"

"Yes, I am the National Chinese Methodist Church Treasurer", he replied.

So, he was an important person who keeps the purse strings of the Chinese Methodist Church, a thriving church in the country.

As it is my habit, I continue with the next statement.

"Oh, so everyone in your family must be a Christian."

"Yes", he replied.

"Everyone?" I remarked, "That is truly wonderful."

He then went on to say, "No, not everyone, because my elderly father has not yet accepted Jesus as his Savior."

"Why not?" I said. "Bring him here and we will share the Good News to him."

"Oh, he does not know I am sick in hospital" he said.

"Tell him, and call us when he comes," I said that and went on with my work.

At 5 p.m. in the evening, the elderly grandfather who was about 85 years of age comes in to visit his son. He speaks the dialect of Hakka, which is very different from my own dialect. I cannot converse in Hakka. They called me and I then called my colleague, Dr Liao who was fluent in Hakka.

"Chee Ming, come along, we have work to do!" I had earlier told him about this elderly man.

We went and saw and spoke to this elderly man. Literally, in fifteen minutes, the senior elderly grandfather gave his life to Jesus. He was actually ready, and a little prompting, a little nudge and some persuasion was all that was needed for him.

Romans 10:13-15 says that "For whoever calls on the name of the LORD shall be saved. How then shall they call on Him whom they have not believed? And how can they believe in Him of whom they have not heard? And how shall they hear without a preacher? And how shall they preach unless they are sent?"

It was a great time of celebration for the family when their grandfather, the last among the generations came to know Jesus.

The next day, I came to see the patient and told him this:

"God works in mysterious and wondrous ways. You and your family have been praying for your father for years. God had to bring you into hospital for us to see you, treat you, and in that process the opportunity to meet and pray for your unsaved dad. Now that he is saved, and you are well, you can go off."

Truly since discharge, I do not recall ever seeing him again.

What have I learned from this testimony?

It is our Father's wish that none should perish – None.

Testimony # 074 "Jesudason came to my Clinic"

This is a very special testimony that I share very often, and one that continues to edify, inspire and encourage me. It is one of those mysterious and strange incidents which I do not fully understand even until today. I will relate it as I remember.

Pastor Jesudason from Malacca brought a young teenager to see me. I remember that his problem was minor and it did not require any further investigations or brain scans.

He had introduced himself as a pastor, and talked about his work and ministry in Malacca, including work with the Portuguese settlement. His family was well and one of his children, his son was working as a doctor.

At the end of the consultation, which took place in Kuala Lumpur, I asked the standard questions, which I ask all the ministers who come to see me.

"How is your church getting on? Is there anything I can do to help?"

He replied and said, "I am all right. However, my senior Pastor Vincent Maniam needs support. A Korean church has been supporting him before, but has stopped their support recently. It would be good if you can help."

"Sure, do give me his number and I will call him and talk to him," I answered, and then saw Pastor Jesudason off.

A week or so later, I called Pastor Maniam, and we made contact and I committed myself to assist him through this period while he was in Malacca, as his earlier support had ceased. We made regular contact over the phone, and soon after, he came over to Kuala Lumpur and we are in contact since.

One day, while he was in Malacca, and we were talking on the phone, he told me that Pastor Jesudason was beside him, and asked whether I wanted to talk to him.

"Sure", I said.

I then spoke to Pastor Jesudason, and within seconds, he interrupted me and said, "Who are you?"

"Oh, I am Dr Timothy Sng from Gleneagles Hospital."

"Oh, I don't think we have met," Pastor Jesudason said politely.

"Oh, you did come to my office once with a teenager for a consultation. And it was you who introduced me to Pastor Maniam" I continued.

"No, it wasn't me" he said.

I left it at that. Maybe, I got mixed up, I thought. I then reflected that there was a man named Pastor Jesudason, and at least that's who he said he was. He did introduce me to Pastor Maniam and even gave me his number. He also told me about himself and his work, and that his son is a doctor. It couldn't be a mistake.

I went back to my clinic records, but could not trace that episode when he came to my office. I did not pursue the matter, but continued to communicate with GISM (the name of the church in Malacca, which stood for Gereja Injil Sepenuh Malacca).

Some months later, I spoke to Pastor Maniam again, and this time I asked if Pastor Jesudason was around. He was, and I asked to be put through to him.

I said, "Pastor Jesudason, good afternoon. How are you? Remember we spoke once before and I was describing to you how we met in my office, and how you introduced me to Pastor Maniam." He replied, "I am really sorry, but I did not come to your office in Kuala Lumpur. I have never been to your hospital before."

I was stunned again. It was then that I decided I should make a trip to Malacca to meet this man called Pastor Jesudason. By now, it must be about a year since that incidence. I travelled down to Malacca as my son was studying there, and together we went to visit Pastor Jesudason. On one of those visits, his grandson has seen Jesus Christ standing beside me, as related in episode or testimony # 003.

When we met face to face, the man before me was a total stranger, whom I have never met before. I related what had happened in Kuala Lumpur and confirmed that the details of the conversation were factually correct.

It was then that Pastor Jesudason related that this was not the first time when he 'visited' someone, though he had not personally done so.

Until this day, I cannot fully understand what happened, except to say that I did meet a Pastor Jesudason and the details of our conversation were correct. Also, the man whom I later got to know as Pastor Jesudason was not the one that I recalled in my memory, as the man who visited me.

So, who came to see me? An angel? Someone who stood in as 'Pastor Jesudason'?

What I believe could have happened is that as he prayed with a serious burden for support for Pastor Maniam, and the Holy Spirit worked to transmit that prayer into a "visitation by Pastor Jesudason" in my office, and his prayers were answered. He was translated to meet me and convey the urgent need to support Pastor Maniam.

I am in my right state of mind, and the points and facts are very clear; someone did come to see me, introducing himself as Pastor Jesudason, spoke with all the points and facts that concern him, and I responded; subsequently, he denies that he came; when I went down to meet him, it seemed that the one who came to see me was not this person, by appearance; who then came to see me then? A supernatural phenomenon had taken place and God's Name is being glorified. I thank God that I can be used by Him for His Glory.

What do I learn from this testimony?

Jesus said in Matthew 25:43, "I was a stranger and you did not take Me in, naked and you did not clothe Me, sick and in prison and you did not visit Me."

God is omnipresent. He visits us when we are unaware. Many supernatural phenomena can happen around us as part of God's plans.

Testimony # 075   The Demon Spoke

This testimony relates the only time I have heard the audible 'voice of a demon', self-acknowledged and speaking directly to me. This testimony is true, and witnessed by me and the parents of the victim-patient concerned.

A 17-year old Chinese teenager from Batu Pahat had come to see me. Batu Pahat is about 240 kilometers from the capital city of Kuala Lumpur, and about 3 hours drive by car, according to Google.

His parents had brought him, as they were desperate about the state of their son. They had been to many doctors, and even brought him to see over a dozen mediums or the equivalent of the Malaysian witch-doctor, without any good response.

"My son has been in a state of stupor, and not been to school for over seven months. We do not know what is wrong with him", his father asserted.

I felt sorry for the boy and his parents, as I empathized with the family. It did not look like any sort of neurological or psychological disorder. I then asked permission from the parents to share with them about Jesus Christ. They nodded.

I gently called out to his name. He looked at me, as I called out to his name. That was a positive sign, because a response to one's name is important.

I then urged him to repeat after me a short sentence of faith and declaration below:

Calling his name again, I asked him if he could say: "Jesus is Lord."

He looked at me and then said softly in Chinese, "Jesus is Lord."

"Wonderful!" I said. "Please say again: 'Jesus is Lord'."

He repeated softly, while looking at me, "Jesus is Lord."

"Great!" I said, encouragingly, "Please say it for the third time".

"Jesus is Lord" he repeated again.

"Fantastic!" I said. "If you can say it so clearly three times, why not invite Jesus as your Lord and Savior. He will help you and heal you."

"Follow me in this prayer."

He then followed me and prayed the sinner's prayer. As soon as he had done so, he stood up voluntarily on his own and dug into his pockets, pulled out some talisman, items which are linked to prayer in the Chinese Temple and threw it down in front of his parents, as a sign of his new faith.

I was surprised as were his parents, and I told the parents that he had done so on his own, in discarding those items.

Barely under a minute after what he did, and having sat down, there was a sudden change in his demeanor as he lapsed into semi-consciousness, closed his eyes and slumped into his chair, though still upright.

I was alone with the victim-patient and both parents as they were witnessing some strange phenomenon right in front of their eyes, as his son had for one moment become normal and alert after the prayer, and next slumped back into his previous state.

I looked at him, but there was no eye contact, as his eyes remained closed. I called out to his name, once, twice and three times, but there was no answer.

I then took control and ask in an authoritative voice: "Who are you!?"

A soft, lady-like voice answered, "I am a demon."

I had never expected to hear this, as it was the first time, I heard an audible voice claiming to be a demon.

Staying calm and in full authority, as it was in my clinic, I stated firmly, "What are you doing inside this person? He now belongs to Jesus!"

The demon replied, "Please, please, please, I have no place to go."

Oddly, I felt pity for a split second, but immediately knew that I could not show pity for that situation.

"No, you cannot stay on there. Where do you come from?"

Again, immediately, a reply came. The demon stated an address, not familiar to me.

Both parents heard and said, "That's the family cemetery!"

I immediately knew I needed help, and called a sister-in-Christ to come down to join me. Both of us sang a short hymn of praise and worship, and prayed for the teenager.

He opened his eyes and was set free.

I rejoiced with the parents and explained what had happened. I urged them to bring the teenager to church.

They went back to their home town of Batu Pahat.

I called them the next day to check on the teenager, and was happy that he remained well.

What have I learned from this testimony?

Jesus came to set the captives free. Many people are trapped and oppressed, even possessed. God by His awesome power can set the people free, to acknowledge and serve Him.

Testimony # 076   Stopping Thunderstorms Using His Name

There is awesome power in Name of Jesus.

In the days of past, the king had absolute power over the nation he ruled. His authority was effectively administered by his royal officials, who displayed and confirmed their authority through the official attire they wore, the ring they on their finger, the seal they carried or a scroll they would open to the crowds. When they say, "As from today, the king orders all his subjects to bow down before this statue", it became law.

In these days, we too have a King, - the King of Heaven, and He is the King of kings. His Name is Jesus, our Savior and Friend, though we should rightfully call Him, King Jesus. All authority on earth and in heaven has been passed to Him.

Our King Jesus has graciously allowed us to use His authority and power, since we have now been born again into The Kingdom of God, as children of God and fellow heirs. His authority is in His Name – the most beautiful Name ever – Jesus.

I shared this with my son, John and as we were driving from Kuala Lumpur to Mantin, a forty-minute drive, there were dark clouds above with heavy thunderstorms pouring down on us. I told John that when we use the Name of Jesus, we can stop the rain and thunderstorms. There were only two of us in the car.

I said to John, "Let me show you the power of the Name of Jesus."

I prayed, "Lord Jesus, please stop the rain, and clear the dark clouds. We pray in Jesus Name." In about a minute or less in driving time, the skies cleared and the rain stopped and the sunlight shone through. "Praise the Lord!" we both declared.

We drove further on, and heavy thunderstorms came back again, pouring down on our windscreen.

Let's pray again John, "Lord Jesus, please stop the rain and thunderstorms. In Jesus Name." Again, barely a minute in our driving, the clouds cleared again, and rain stopped and the sun shone through.

This happened a total of five more times, and we prayed and stopped the rain a total of seven times, and arrived at our destination with a sunny sky above.

I was not testing the LORD, but in all humility was showing my son the power of the Name of Jesus, which we must not use in vain.

I will relate just one more situation, out of several when I had to walk to my daughter's apartment for the station. The rain was a tropical storm, the sort that does not stop for an hour at least usually. I had faith and believed that the Name of Jesus would stop the rain, and I needed to be back soon at her apartment soon.

I bought an umbrella at the store on the station and still possess that particular umbrella today. I stood at the glass window, and took out my phone and made a short video clip and then prayed using our Lord's Name. Within five minutes, the rain stopped, and I walked home arriving safely. Just outside her apartment, I took a picture showing the wet pavement but no rain.

His awesome, mighty and precious Name is above all Names, and storms, rain, earthquake, typhoons, anything on earth can be stopped or moved by His Mighty Name, the Name of Jesus.

What have I learned from this testimony?

I share with everyone including loved ones who have not yet called upon the Name of Jesus: "If ever you are desperately in trouble, call upon the Name of Jesus. He will save you."

Testimony # 077 God Speaks Through His Word & Prophecies

Hearing God's voice is a part of the Christian walk.

Our God is alive, and He can be heard, if not seen. While not everyone can get to see God, or Jesus, I believe wholeheartedly that everyone should be able to hear from God.

God speaks to us in so many ways. The emphasis of this testimony is that God speaks through His Word and His prophecies, particularly when in crisis or in urgent need.

In earlier testimonies, I referred to the several situations when God spoke in an audible voice, in the still small voice, and sometimes out of the blue.

He uses His servants to speak to His people and His children through the preaching of His Word, through our own reading of the Word during our quiet time with Him, and also through the personal prophecies spoken through His servants.

These words have been a guiding light, a compass in my life and direction.

Hearing God's voice is so important so that we do not go astray, choose the wrong route or path or falter along the way. When we have a clear "go ahead", all things will work out smoothly.

This ministry and passion of writing has been growing within me for over two decades. I recall two particular prophetic words that encouraged me to push on to write and publish. The first was given by Pastor Cherian from Kerala, when he prayed for me and declared, "You will write books." He then paused and asked whether I have already published any. He went on to say that they would be translated into multiple languages.

The next word of prophecy came from Pastor Crystal who saw God grant me four keys, of which one of them was a "Golden Pen" for writing.

When both prophecies were mentioned, I knew in my heart that it would come to pass. My eBooks were published from 2004 onwards. For some reasons, time just flew by so fast, that it would be another ten to fifteen years, before the first book "The Good Son" came out in print in April 2019.

This title "The Testimony of Jesus", Releasing the spirit of prophecy through Awesome Christian Testimonies & Stories" is scheduled to be out on Amazon in November or in print by early December 2019.

There were also two little scares when I was warned. One was about a decade ago, when I heard that "If you do write, I will raise someone else to do so!". It appeared a stern warning, and I responded quickly with over a dozen e-books published about ten years since. The next warning or caution was from a Pastor JD who said that I need to focus.

This title was not planned, neither was "The Good Son", but all sprung up over a few months, and this author truly believes that God's plan is coming to pass. By 2020, no less than six books will be published.

Thus for this author's life, apart from work as a doctor, neurologist, the simultaneously role as a marketplace minister in ushering souls into the Kingdom of God, praying for healing and deliverance, counselling people and supporting the itinerant ministers, apart from serving in the local churches and teaching and preaching along the way, even as a camp speaker and dinner speaker.

Yet, the main passion, ministry and God-directed role is writing. And if God has given the Word through His prophets, these books will reach out to the ends of the earth, for this is His work, His ministry and all are for His Glory.

What can I say about the multiple personal prophecies on my life?

Proverbs 16:9 "A man's heart plans his way. But the LORD directs his steps." I still remember another version which says, "many are the plans of man, and it is God who

directs our steps.” Commit your ways to the LORD, and your thoughts will be established. Those are all one's plans under God's watching eyes. If we commit our work and ministry for God to Him, He will bring it to pass.

“The steps of a good man are ordered by the LORD. And He delights in his way.” Psalms 37;26

The prophet comes along and speaks the words of prophecy that confirm all the plans above.

Testimony # 078 “Reject Your Sickness”

Hearing the various testimonies of my patients have also encouraged me and given me new understanding in praying for the sick.

This gentleman was in his middle fifties, when he suddenly presented with a severe infection of the blood, affecting his conscious level and requiring ventilation, or breathing support by a machine.

He was so critically ill, that he was in the Intensive Care Unit for about ten days. I was his doctor. He was single, and it was his siblings who visited him.

Day by day, he remained unconscious while very strong antibiotics were used to combat the severe infection. He was somehow next to the young lady who came out of coma miraculously, and had a visitation by Jesus the next day.

My faith level was very high following that lady's miraculous resurrection. I believed together with the siblings that this gentleman (we shall call him Mr. Tan) would recover.

On the eighth day, he was well enough to be taken out of the ventilator, but still had lines and a nasogastric tube in. I took the opportunity to quickly talk to him and pray.

This is what he said:

“When I was ill, I knew that I was very sick and dying. Suddenly, I heard a voice. It was Jesus. He spoke to me in a clear and loud voice, “Do not accept your illness. Reject it.”

“That was what Jesus said.”

He smiled and was full of life, just barely a few hours out of the machine, and a week being critically ill.

I took those words to mean that while the LORD was with him, the battle had to come from him too, and his position should be to be strong, not to give up, and to reject the illness.

He was very well a month after the illness, when he came to see me in the clinic.

What have I learned from this testimony?

Never give up! Never give up! Never give up! Reject your illness, reject cancer, reject your infirmity, in Jesus Name. We have authority over sickness, over situations and over almost everything on earth, if we have faith and love.

Do not let the enemy rob us of our rights and blessings.

Testimony # 079   100% Offering Returned

Over the years, nearly four decades now in the LORD, I have been faithful in tithing and giving generously.

One principle that I have is that I almost never to refuse help, when the seeker is genuine and I have the means to help.

This philosophy and principle come from the parable and stories that are related by Jesus, about "not been given water, when he was thirsty" and the "man who called upon his neighbor" in the night. [Matthew 25:42 "for I was hungry and you gave Me no food; I was thirsty and you gave Me no drink; Proverbs 3:28 "Do not say to your neighbor. 'Go, and come back; and tomorrow, I will give it' when you have it.

In both situations, the emphasis is that one should give that glass of water, and the neighbor should respond to help within his or her means.

Another principle in the Bible is that "he who gives to the poor, lends to God", and may I add that God always fulfills his repayment and often blesses extra.

[Proverbs 19:17 "He who has pity on the poor, lends to the LORD."

Over the years, this marketplace ministry has assisted ministers, especially itinerant ministers and servants of the LORD; it is not me alone but with some ten other generous donors, in supporting various ministries.

What is the reaping from all that sowing?

I testify to the Glory of God, that all that I have given to the LORD has been returned to me in full, and more, not through my own earnings or hard work, but through a generous support by a foundation for my personal family needs, amounting to the tune of a million Malaysian ringgit.

I wholeheartedly thank God, with my head bowed to the ground for His goodness and faithfulness.

This testimony is true, and I am totally convinced that you and I cannot out-give God. God is faithful and He supplies all our needs.

I affirm and declare that "in all my four decades as a Christian, all that I have given to God has been returned to me, and more", and all that I have earned, I have effectively kept for myself and my own family's needs. God has used me as a channel of blessings to other, and in return, He has channeled blessings to me and more to come, because when He is faithful.

In giving, I did not expect it to return to me, but was just faithfully "sowing" into the Kingdom of God, and the harvest was abundant and poured back into my coffers.

What do I learn from this four-decade long experience in giving and sharing?

We can never out-give God. We do not wait till we are as rich as Bill Gates before we give generously. The lady with two mites, gave more than the whole congregation. The principle of sowing and reaping is so true and real. Unless we sow, we will never be able to reap.

Also, it is always better to be a lender and giver rather than to be a borrower.

Pray like this: "LORD, make me a giver and lender, and not a borrower."

Testimony # 080   God's Eraser – From One to Seven Distinctions

This relates to my son's academic performance.

Many believers will testify that it is by God's grace that they passed, or did well or managed to enter college or University, and get a good job.

This testimony is about my son John. He was about to sit for the "O" levels examinations, this being the secondary school examinations before the pre-University studies. It was customary for the school to give a forecast of the student's potential performance in the formal examinations that was about to take place. As these formal results would take some time, colleges use forecast results to admit students, and confirm their status when the actual results come out.

John had a forecast of "one" single distinction. This is considered below par or poor, as many would be given 6, 7, 8 or even up to 10 distinctions, if they sit for that many papers or subjects.

For some reason, his performance had dwindled over recent years. As the first born male, he was always different if not special. Do read the next testimony # 081 The First-Born Male is Mine. I had complete peace about him, his direction, his purpose, his plans in life, because, as I thought and believed, "He belongs to the LORD", and hence was His problem, and He will look after him.

We in the family, looked at the forecast and literally 'laughed', whether in despair or in doubt or in sheer surprise. However, when the actual results came out, he had seven distinctions, which is not the best but was good enough to enable him to proceed onwards, and eventually graduate with a medical degree.

I am convinced, and have often said so to him, that THE LORD used His eraser and changed the result from one to seven!

Praise the LORD!!!

What have I learned from this testimony?

God can turn failure into success. He is always on our side.

Testimony # 081 "The First-Born Male is Mine"

My first child Grace was born in July 1981, and it was during my wonderful journey seeking God, that culminated with my salvation on the 18th of October 1981.

Her name coincidentally was Grace, given by me and my wife, at a time when we did not know what the meaning of Grace was. In fact, it was Grace's difficult pregnancy, requiring my wife Jane to be in hospital for complete bed rest for a full three months. It was perhaps this admission, that had triggered me to search for the Living God. Grace had led me to Grace!

In 1986, my wife and I was expecting our second child, and we knew through the ultrasound examination that the child would be a boy.

One day, out of the blue, the LORD spoke to me and said, "This first-born male is mine. Give him to Me. His name is John."

I was surprised and excited that the LORD had spoken and even given him his name.

Two of my heroes in the faith are two great men from China. One is Watchman Nee, who writings I have been following, while the other is John Sung, the great evangelist, who came to Malaya and led many people, especially the indigenous Chinese to Christ.

So, indeed, I was excited to know that my first-born male will be called "John", whose name will be so close to the great evangelist of China and Asia, "John Sung".

I checked out the Scriptures.

Exodus 34:19 "All that open the womb are Mine, and every male firstborn among the livestock."

Exodus 13:2 "Consecrate to Me all the firstborn, whatever opens the womb among the children of Israel of man and beast; it is Mine."

Exodus 22:29 "You shall not delay to offer the first of your ripe produce and your juices. The firstborn of your sons, you shall give to Me."

That was a clear Scripture teaching, which I did not really know, nor is it being taught or practiced consistently in church. We are talking about giving, not just dedicating to the LORD, - a 100% giving back to God, as Hannah gave Samuel back to God.

Next, was the verse, "His name is John."

Right around the same time, a sister intercessor Eleanor called me and said that the LORD gave her a verse from Luke, which said, "His name is John." [Luke 1:63]

I had also felt in my spirit that it was the John the Baptist that my firstborn male was being named after, and not the apostle John.

I kept that word from the LORD in my heart, and did not share it with anyone, including my wife, for I was afraid that she would object to the name 'John' if I had told the name earlier.

I thus gave John to the LORD from the time he was in the womb of my wife.

John was born by normal birth at University Hospital on the 21st of October 1986. Even his arrival was full of drama. My wife suddenly faced contractions and needed to be on some medication, or salbutamol. Her heart rate went quite irregular, with alternating ectopics, or abnormal heart beats. We were concerned about her heart, and wanted a closer monitoring in University Hospital, under the same obstetrician, Professor Siva.

We made an urgent decision to fly to Kuala Lumpur from Kuching. My wife, Jane did not look pregnant, and we took the risk and flew over the day before John was born, without any problems, as a loose blouse was enough to cover the pregnancy.

John was born the next day in Kuala Lumpur.

Jane then asked me what we should call him.

I said," His name is John!"

John Sng or Dr John Sng's story is only 33 years at the time of publication, and it has not yet really started. It will be another story, told by him, perhaps.

Asia, and the world is still waiting for the arrival of another John Sung, in the form of perhaps one like my (or God's) John Sng or one of the youths and young men and women out there. Why just one "John Sung" when there are potentially thousands upon thousands of evangelists, teachers, prophets, pastors and apostles that can be made ready to be sent out into the world.

My country is unique because we have a big population of fluent speakers of English, Mandarin, Malay, Indonesian and Tamil, enough to reach out to half of the world's population.

Fathers and mothers, have you given your first-born male to the LORD. Do so today.

What have I learned from this testimony?

God is still waiting for your firstborn male to be given back to Him.

Testimony # 082   Falling Off an Escalator

God protects us in many situations, probably every day, if not every moment.

I was travelling in Spain, and had just arrived back in Madrid by bullet train from Valencia. It was a big train station, and confusing too, because more than one train can depart from the same platform. I was travelling with my wife. Each of us had a medium size luggage to tug along. My first error was entering a wrong train, and thankfully, we got out in the nick of time. We were told that the regular train into the city would depart from that particular platform. Seeing a solitary train there, we entered and were 'relieved' we were on time. Something told me to check and to my 'shock', we were in a fast train heading out of Madrid! If the train had moved, we would have been travelers without a ticket, to a destination that we did not plan to go.

We jumped out and headed for the information center.

This was when I fell off the escalator backwards. I had a medium sized luggage with me. Obviously, one should not place it in front as the escalator moved. I had to decide whether to put it on my right side or behind me. Not wanting to obstruct people who may want to walk up fast, I did what most people would do, place the medium sized luggage behind me.

As soon, as we went up the escalator, the luggage tilted backwards due to friction over the moving edge in front of it. My right hand was behind me, holding on the luggage handle.

That tilt and tug backwards was enough to pull me back and off balance. I immediately fell backwards. Like most falls, it is almost in slow-motion. My bump fell on the center of the bag or luggage, and that buffered me significantly, with my back on the long handle protecting me from the sharp edges of the escalator, while my head was floating over the moving steps.

For some unexplained reason, probably because of the long handle of the bag still being at the edge of the base, I was still close to the first step. An inner voice told me to kick backwards and get off the escalator. I found myself kicking and was safely off the escalator at the bottom on safe ground.

By that time, my wife was up on the floor above, stunned and staring at what had happened to me. My luggage was midway up the escalator, while I was lying flat on the floor. Two Spanish men rushed to help, one going for my luggage, and the other towards me.

I felt well except for some bruises on my elbow. I said, "Thank you, I am all right."

The other men passed my luggage to my wife. Both were not railway staff, and we were touched by their assistance.

Up until this day, I cannot understand how I was able to get off the escalator and was safe on the ground below.

Like the drifting away in the Pacific Ocean, I was reminded of the danger that I was in, I could have smashed my head badly or suffered a deep gash. Thank God indeed, from the depths of my heart.

On my return back home, someone send me a video of a CEO who fell off the escalator, smashed his head, and kept rolling backwards on and on, on the escalator and died in his own building!

And he was upright, reading his mobile phone, when he steps backwards accidentally and had a tragic fatal fall.

Clearly, again the LORD, through my angels must have protected me from injury, whether a fracture, a head injury or even death.

I counted so far, some eight times when my life was in danger – this fall being one of them, apart from the drifting in the ocean, the near hit by the fire engine, the miss by the runaway lorry, the bulging tire, the smashing of my head on the bedroom floor, my exposure with a deadly virus, and my undiagnosed heart artery blockage.

I thank God for saving my life, sparing me of injury, which could even have left me paralyzed.

I got up with minimal bruises and continued with my journey as though nothing had happened. God is good and faithful, and His steadfast love for me is everlasting.

What can I say about this testimony?

I am forever thankful to my LORD, for He is my protector and my shield.

Testimony # 083   Patients Stories – Attacked by Demons

I continue to learn from the experiences of my patients.

This first one is about a sister in Christ who came in for a minor illness. For two nights in a row, in the double-bedded room she was in, she had nightmares for two consecutive nights, walking through darkness, with eerie spirits around. She asked the nursing sister, a believer for advice, and the sister summoned me for help to pray for her.

I entered her room, introduced myself and prayed for covering for the room. She slept peacefully for the next night, giving Glory to God.

I have learned from this and other testimonies to pray whenever I am in a new place. I have experienced at least three incidents myself in hotel rooms, and hospital on call rooms, when I overlooked praying for the room. In one instance, I had a horrible dream of death, blood and dead bodies. This was in a hospital on call room. I checked the next day, and was told that during the Japanese Occupation, many people were killed in that place. As for hotel room, on one instance in the middle of the night, a dark figure appeared next to my bed. I sat up at once and prayed in Jesus Name and peace came.

One male patient complained to me the next day, that the nurse had insisted he get up and walk although he was not well, and was recovering from an operation. This was in the intensive care unit. I investigated and found no truth in this accusation, as the nurse did not do so. The next night, the same patient related how a team of three or four came in and started to interrogate him, and even tied and beat him up. It was a terrifying experience for him.

It was the second night's incidence that clearly told me that these were visitation by 'resident spirits. I prayed with the Intensive Care Unit's chief nurse and claimed and declared a peaceful and safe environment for the ICU. For a season all was well and peaceful after that.

In the same ICU, another middle-aged lady complained that one night she was harassed attacked and assaulted, including having her head smashed against the wall. She wanted to go home urgently the next day, after relating her experience. We had to let her go home, as her condition had stabilized.

It is my practice now to include prayer, especially for very ill patients. It makes a difference – a lot of difference.

What have I learned about this story?

The unclean spirits are everywhere. Pray without ceasing, for protection and the LORD's Hand upon our lives and our families. Praying in tongues covers areas that we are not even aware of. For we battle not against flesh and blood, but the powers and principalities, and it is the LORD who fights for us.

Testimony # 084   Survived Knife Attack – over a dozen stitches

I have heard several testimonies how the name of Jesus is so powerful. See # 001, for example.

My cousin was attacked by a `parang' wielding robber, the 'parang' being a short sword used regularly for clearing tropical forests.

He screamed the name of Jesus, fell down bleeding, and was in pain. The attacker fled without taking his wallet. The Name of Jesus is powerful.

My cousin Steven survived though he needed over a dozen stitches.

Two of my other friends too were attacked by robbers, and both called upon Jesus, and suffered minor injuries, and their lives spared, with the robbers leaving without any loot. One took place as he was going for a Cell meeting. The attacker slashed his shoulder area and took off with the car, which was left nearby. This brother said he did not feel any pain at all, though he was bleeding.

In the other situation, the robbers entered the home, and the wife cried out to Jesus. Somehow only the man of the house was injured as a finger was slashed but not amputated. The robbers ran off, and accidentally dropped their bag into the house. Nothing was stolen, and the finger was stitched with full recovery.

What do we learn from these attacks?

Be careful!! Nevertheless, when in danger, always call upon our God, for He is our protector and my shield.

Testimony # 085   In the Nick of Time (Train in Paris)

It was our first trip to Paris, and we had our infant daughter Grace with us.

It was a short trip of just two or three days, and we managed to find a cheap room, then only 10 USD per day right in the middle of the city. This was in the early eighties, when air B&B, and the internet had not yet arrived.

We made a mistake of placing our luggage in the train station we arrived in as the departing station was different.

I wanted very much to see the Sacred Heart Church, but time was limited. On coming out of the station, I realized that it was quite a long way up to the beautiful church. And the train was due to leave on the dot, barely an hour away.

That left me with only one option. I told my wife to proceed to the station and wait for us, while I ran up to have a glimpse of the church at close range. I then ran down, and rushed to the station where our luggage was kept.

It was a task to find the office for "Left Luggage" and to those who know Paris, travelling with luggage along the Metro can be quite a task as the walking distance between stations can be very far.

That left me with only one choice, - to take a cab. I took a cab, knowing that I was short of cash, and embarrassingly paid less that the fare, as I rushed off into the train station.

I was literally rushing and running and barely got up onto the train before it moved. It was two or three seconds, five at the most, when I stepped my foot into the train and it left.

My wife and child were inside. I cannot imagine how messy it would have been, if they had left without me.

The LORD saved me from unnecessary trouble, and really helped me and my family during our 17-day trip in Europe. I recall also that the trip, involving flying one leg only cost less than USD 400 for everything.

What have I learned from this testimony?

Our angels watch over us! I have no doubt the many times THE LORD has assisted me through tight situations. It was scary, maybe silly. He knows how reckless, careless and foolish we are so often. Perhaps when we hear His voice more often, we will make less risky decisions.

Testimony # 086   Walking in Dark Tunnel/ Driving Through Floods

The Dark Tunnel

I joined my daughter in her church camp, when I visited her one year.

It was a lively church, and I had a wonderful few days with the 'family of Christ'.

This short testimony is about my first-time experience of walking in a dark tunnel, which was part of the many waterways in the United Kingdom. It was on a bright sunny day, as we went for this walk during one of the afternoons, as part of the camp activity.

We had to walk along one tunnel. It was dark, and the floor was slippery, and none of us had a torch light! There was however a safety railing at the edge of the path for us to hold on to, though it was rusty and rough. I had my young daughter beside me holding my arm, but it was still scary. Psalm 23 came to my mind, "even though I walk through the valley of the shadow of death!"

I do not remember praying on this occasion, as I was focusing on my path.

God knew for sure as just about ten yards along and into the tunnel, a barge with a low light came from the other side at a distance, lightening up the tunnel a little.

It immediately gave me some light, and confidence to walk through the now dimly lit tunnel for the first half of the journey as the barge was slow, rather than a pitch-black journey, which took probably about ten minutes. Midway, light from the other end helped as the barge went past us.

I thank the LORD for His timely light.

The Floods

On another occasion back in Malaysia, while coming back from the east coast state of Terengganu, we encountered floods. We arrived near a town called Maran in Pahang, on the way back to Kuala Lumpur, when there was shallow flood, probably about a foot deep at the most.

We could not check how the floods were down the road, and there was no feedback from travelers. Again, these are the days before the internet. Also, hotels and bed and breakfast centers were few then, especially in the country side. It was about 5.30 p.m. in the evening, and we were driving a normal 1300 cc Japanese car, borrowed from my brother-in-law.

I decided to brave the floods as we drove on without difficulty through this first flood. A few kilometers further on, I was shocked to see a sea of water in front of us, with no indication where the road was.

What should one do in such a situation? The correct thing to do would have been to back off, turn back and put up for a night at the nearest hotel or motel. I was young and brash in my early thirties.

There were a crowd of boys, who were helping vehicles cross the "sea." Vehicles were still crossing on both sides of the "sea", assisted by these boys for a small fee. Like a fool, I decided that we could do it. I hired the boys, who told us to switch off the engine, while they placed a rubber mat across the radiator, and the gear was put free. In the car were me, my wife and my mother-in-law in the back seat with my infant daughter Grace.

We proceeded with the young lads pushing the car, and right at the lowest point of the road we saw a lorry coming from the other side almost along our path. The boys narrowly steered us on the right path just avoiding the lorry as we moved on to the other side.

Then suddenly, water started entering the car from both sides and our feet became soaked with muddy water. We did not have any bowls or containers to scoop the water out. All we could do was use 'sarongs', a loose form of lower gown to scoop water out.

It was a terrifying experience, but we made it on dry ground above. I paid the boys and then prayed that I could start the car, while all our feet were soaked wet with muddy water.

I thank God for His intervention. I turn the keys on and within seconds, I heard a healthy engine purring and we drove on, and back to Kuala Lumpur.

The car, with its carpet soaked required a proper cleaning and servicing, and the stench continued for weeks. Thankfully, my brother-in-law was not too upset that his car had a good soak in muddy water.

What did I learn from these two harrowing experiences?

I am assured that God is always there with us, even when we take risks, and are in dangerous situations. However, I know that we should not keep taking risks, because sooner or later, we may run out of "Grace & Mercy."

Testimony # 087   Traffic Jams & Miraculous Trips

There are countless situations when we are stuck desperately in a traffic jam, and our prayers got us to our destination on time.

My daughter Grace in her Tour of the United States with her fellow Bible College students, travelling in a van would consistently sing praises to the LORD, and they would be on time for their performance at the churches they were visiting. She would sing the same chorus from Darlene Zschech's Hillsong song, "Shout to the LORD", and they made it each time, even in the busy streets of New York.

Try it:

Shout to the Lord all the Earth, let us sing
Power and majesty, praise to the King
Mountains bow down and the seas will roar
At the sound of Your name

I will shall just recount three situations, the first two being really urgent and the third being an amazing demonstration of His Mighty Hand.

I was late, and the fault was purely mine. I had exactly twenty minutes to drive from home to the Main Lecture Hall where I was chairing an International Conference in Neurology. The distance from my home to the hotel would have normally taken 20-30 minutes, without a traffic jam, and more if the traffic was heavy. Besides, the conference hall was situated on the 11th floor of this hotel, called Berjaya Times Square.

As I drove, I prayed without ceasing, simultaneously making contact with a medical representative to take my car at the front lobby while I raced into the Hotel with barely a minute to spare, all flustered and 'stressed'. I made it just in time, and until today, cannot recall why I made such a silly mistake of leaving home late.

The LORD saved me from embarrassment and shame.

For the second situation, I was scheduled to speak at a Christian Medical Event on a Saturday afternoon. I rushed off after work with about forty minutes to spare to get to the church where the meeting was held, perhaps 30 kilometers away. I recall I was about ten minutes away by car, and about ten kilometers in distance away. Again, I was praying without ceasing and arrived, park and entered the church hall just in time. I was less stressed for this meeting, as being late for a few minutes was not so crucial, but I recalled that traffic appeared heavy, but suddenly moved.

In this third situation recently, I was at another hospital visiting someone, when I was scheduled to begin my clinic at 2 p.m. or in nine minutes time. I was already on the road, and using Waze driving along the highway, the expected time of arrival was in 22 minutes, which meant that I would be 14 minutes late, as Waze noted ETA as 2.14 p.m.

I drove faster and saw the ETA drop to 2.13 p.m. For that relatively short journey, and traffic was heavy, the most I could have saved in travelling time would usually be 2 minutes, i.e. from 22 to 20 minutes, from all my experience driving in the streets of Kuala Lumpur.

Something within me prompted me to pray and say, "God can shave off 5 minutes easily; with God all things are possible." I did not have the faith to look at Waze, nor at the clock, but felt something strange within me that THE LORD was going to show me His Amazing Hand.

The roads suddenly became clear and traffic was smooth, while I still drove within speed limits. I still felt that even with smooth traffic and no jam, it would really take a miracle to shave off 5 minutes from the expected time of arrival.

I testify (The LORD is my witness) that I reached the very site of my hospital entrance at 2.08 p.m. a good 6 minutes earlier than expected.

The LORD had shaved off 6 minutes miraculously from a journey that was supposed to be 22 minutes! I was stunned, amazed and shocked, and after my clinic that same day, I bowed down in awe, with head to the floor (ground) of my office worshipping my LORD.

I believe wholeheartedly that THE LORD did it for me so that I can testify to His Amazing Hand here in this book.

What can we take away from the above testimonies?

God, our Father is just so awesome! His Majestic Hand upon our lives, Father's Presence, Jesus beside us, and the Holy Spirit in us, with our personalized angels around us means that we can conquer mountains, cross the oceans, and storm the valleys.

Testimony # 088   Running out of Gas (Petrol)

Again, in my younger days, the dangerous things we do are silly and should not be done.

I travelled with my petrol running on a lowish tank. I really wonder now why I took such risks. It was the last stretch on the East Coast link to Kuala Lumpur. There are not many gas or petrol stations along the way then, especially on the highland stretch near Genting.

I had reached the highest point and the dial showed "E", for empty. "E" can mean really zero for Continental cars, while for Japanese cars, it may still have some reserve.

Whether there was reserve or not in my Toyota, I am not so sure now, but we were certainly running low on petrol, and there was no petrol station for at least twenty kilometers.

I prayed and trusted God, pleading for His Mercy and we arrived safely near home, just in time to fill the gas tank again.

The miracle was that the dial hardly lowered throughout the drive, giving me confidence that we would make to home safely.

I now make sure that there is always enough petrol in the tank, and generally pump in petrol when the dial is down to 20-25 %.

What do I learn from this testimony?

We must plan better. God is forever faithful, and provides for all our needs, but we must not test Him or unnecessarily risk our lives.

Testimony # 089   Exposed to a Deadly Virus

We have heard of medical personnel succumbing to dangerous bugs. The Ebola and SARS stories are scary. Apparently, every two years, a new virus arrives.

I was looking after a patient with severe brain encephalitis, with typical features of rhombencephalitis, and clinically had hydro phobia and seizures. The provisional diagnosis was obviously a "Rabies Encephalitis", and the Brain MRI showed that he was unlikely to survive the illness. He lived in a region where there were still rabid animals.

I made a mistake or was careless. While examining him closely, his saliva fell on my thumb, and I had an open wound on it.

That meant that if he had rabies, I could die too!

I checked and searched for the antibodies for rabies, but it was not available in Kuala Lumpur or in Bangkok, where rabies was still endemic. I had no choice but to use the vaccine, and gave myself the vaccine.

I prayed and then waited, day by day.

Although, the tests came back negative for the patient, he died. He had the typical features that point towards a bad virus attack on the brain.

I survived, but then suffered from Posterior Uveitis possibly as a result of the vaccine, and I went on to have a retinal detachment and the drama around it, when it happened in Japan. See # testimony 020 where I relate about my retinal detachment.

God protected me and saved me from a potentially deadly virus.

What can we learn from this testimony?

We give thanks that God is always there in times of danger. Psalm 91 is a good word that declares the foundation of our protection and faith.

Testimony # 090   Open Doors & God's Favor – Study in UK

It was in 1985, when I was offered a scholarship by the British Council to study Neurology.

I needed approval from my Director General before I could go for the one-year study. My first application was rejected.

Though young in faith, I trusted that prayers to my LORD would move mountains. I believed that my scholarship would be followed by an approval by the Ministry of Health, or the Director General. I called the Ministry and was told that I could not meet the Director General. That meant that my options were nearly zero.

I prayed for God's favor and open doors. My state director called me, and told me that the Director General was coming over to visit Kuching, and I could talk to him over the lunch period.

That was when I had earlier donated RM 800, the cost of my flight to Kuala Lumpur towards the purchase of a church van. I told the LORD that rather than fly to KL and waste that funds, I would give it to the church towards a much-needed church van.

The big boss came, had lunch and while I was thinking how I could approach him, he actually walked directly towards me, as though there was a magnetic force around me.

I immediately introduced myself and told him that I was the one who needed his approval to go to the United Kingdom for further studies in Neurology.

He called my director over to where we were and asked him whether he could release me to further my studies.

He (Datuk Stalin) said, "Yes!"

The Director General then turned to me and said, "Okay, I will approve your leave by next week."

Hallelujah! Praise the LORD!

I knew then and there that it was the LORD who had opened the doors. He had brought the man over, and softened his heart, and it was an approval on the spot.

The next miracle that followed was that I was only 6 weeks from the start of the course, and in that short period, I was able to get a good accommodation in a special hostel meant for Asians postgraduate doctors, at a nominal sum of only 65 Sterling pounds a month.

My wife Jane, and toddler Grace, now about four years packed our bags for the second trip to UK. It was probably this trip that made Grace fall in love with Britain and subsequently spent a good eight years abroad in Britain and Canada.

This postgraduate study for over a year was to be a very important stepping stone that allowed me to practice in neurology for the past 27 years. The LORD knew how important it was for my life and career, and intervened for me.

Hallelujah! Praise the LORD!

What have I learned from this episode?

Trust the LORD always. The truth is that God will open doors, provide opportunities and is with us through every step of our life and journey.

Testimony # 091   Police Report & Complaints Against me

Practice in medicine is full of challenges in recent times, and one even hears of assault and injury on medical personnel when things go wrong.

What about someone who shares the Gospel freely, and prays for the sick very often? Yes, I was shouted at by the atheist, and spit at by a close relative. I have also nearly been complained against to the Ministry of Health for sharing the Gospel, but in all the above and including the situation below, God has bailed me out.

This short testimony is about a patient who was mentally unwell, and possibly even under some spiritual oppression.

I was asked to give a second opinion. I entered a dark room, with a low light, and the patient was wearing shades. After a short interview, I sensed that there were deep psychological issues, and possibly some spiritual elements.

I spoke positively and assuredly to her, and encouraged her and family. Her husband and wo children were around. I tapped her arms and legs as part of the assessment and she did react with some pain.

There seemed no issues about my assessment.

That night, her husband made a police report against me stating that "I had hit his wife!"

The hospital "Complaints Officer" had called a meeting the next day for me to meet the husband and family.

I thought the whole matter was just ridiculous. Nevertheless, a police report was made against me, and technically, the investigating officer could come in and arrest me for further investigation and place me on remand or jail up to two weeks.

Imagine the headlines on the front page, "Doctor accused of assaulting patient."

I immediately took steps to protect myself, calling my lawyer friend, and police department contacts to neutralize these false accusations.

And of course, I prayed and sent out requests for intercession from my fellowship members and intercessors.

Within the week, the case was closed. I did not need to be interviewed by the police.

I never saw the patient or her family after that.

What have I learned from this situation?

Accusations against the believer continue in the courts of Heaven. Be aware that the story of Job is not only in the past. It is still happening today, and the courts in Heaven is busy with tons of accusations by the accuser. Read Richard Henderson's books on this area.

Testimony # 092   Three Weeks Honeymoon with Jesus

In the year 2014, I decided to take three weeks off from work, society and my hectic city life to a mountain village called Bario.

Bario is situated in the Highlands of Sarawak, Malaysia, in one of the largest islands of the world called Borneo. Borneo is a fascinating place to visit and live it, and my family and I had the privilege of living there for four years.

Sarawak is also my spiritual kindergarten where I spent my earlier Christian years, soaking in the word and enriched by the fellowship of saints from the city of Kuching, named after the cat.

As for Bario, it is the village from which my God parents come from, the homeland of the Kelabit people. Historically, from the Christian point of view, it is the where the Bario Revival of the early seventies took place.

With that background, Bario was indeed the ideal place for me to take a three-week isolated retreat to be with "Jesus". It was to be my "Honeymoon with Jesus", a title that I have begun to write based on my daily diary. To take a three weeks' time off from one's wife, and from work is a significant thing, and worth a book by itself.

This testimony is more a story, and though there may not be a specific happening, the three weeks was indeed "a major happening" in my life. Originally meant to be "my personal retreat", it turned out to be a very special time between me and my Lord.

This is the story.

Just before take-off, a sudden sense of remorse and sadness filled my soul, as I realized that this is my first ever "honeymoon with Jesus". I have not dedicated time for Him, to be alone with my Lord. Imagine, being married for over 34 years, and yet have not really spend a dedicated time like a honeymoon with your beloved.

There was a short stop over at Miri airport and then we took off in a Twin Otter to Bario. It was a good day, and I could see a famous landmark, a fingertip mountain structure known as The Alchetron or Bukit Batu Lawi, a fingertip-like peak pointing to the heavens.

On arrival in Bario, I automatically went down on my knees and kissed the ground. I had arrived on a special retreat, literally shut off from the world, and just dedicated to my LORD. Lucy Labang was there to greet me; and she and David were to be my hosts for the next three weeks.

I divided the three weeks into three parts. The first part being a 'debriefing for myself', the next being for my Lord, and the third being plans for the future. With WIFI at a minimal and telephone reception very poor, my isolation in this retreat was enforced effectively.

It was a time dedicated to prayer, thinking, writing, planning and meditating on the WORD of God. Time does not permit me to go into details, as the content of the three weeks will be in a separate title, "Three Weeks with Jesus."

No, I did not see Jesus, nor did I hear Him audibly, nor did I dream of Him, but because I dedicated the time to the LORD, God in His faithfulness was there.

One key lesson or message was that at the end of the second week, the Holy Spirit impressed me to change the focus on the last and third week to the Holy Spirit. That was a major shift in direction and focus.

It suddenly impressed on me that I have a very special "Guest of Honor" in my "House", who is none other than the third Person of the Holy Trinity. He was invited into my "House" wholeheartedly when I gave my life to the LORD, and welcomed Jesus as my Lord and Savior. The Spirit of Christ (aka The Holy Spirit & the Spirit of God) entered me, and I was born again as a child of God, and the Holy Spirit now dwells in me.

What has happened since? He has been a 'silenced' Guest, not a silent Guest, for He has spoken from time to time, and I had not graciously allowed Him to speak more often.

I repented and asked the Holy Spirit to be center in my life, and to be a part of my thought life, my Counselor, Teacher, Guide and Adviser.

My last week was interrupted when a dear friend passed away suddenly, and I returned early, a few days short. My 'honeymoon' with Jesus will be continued at the end of this year, after this book is published with another week, just me and Jesus, somewhere in the mountains of my beloved nation.

I definitely focused on my faith, my walk with the LORD, and my relationship with my Savior Jesus. Drawing closer to the LORD meant that He draws near to me. The greatest of all commandments is to love God, with all our heart, all our might, all our mind and all our soul.

One major renewal that took place in these three weeks was the restoration of the Holy Spirit as Guest of Honor in my life, in my physical temple.

What is so special about spending time with The LORD?

Indeed, when you draw near to God, He will draw near to you. [James 4:8] Have you had your `honeymoon' with Jesus, your quiet personal retreat with Jesus?

Testimony # 093   Jesus, Son of God, - Most Powerful Name

This book is all about Jesus, - "The Testimony of Jesus".

"Who is Jesus" is the ultimate question that gives us the ultimate answer of the whole Universe, and what life and all around our life on earth is about.

Thus, these next eight testimonies are different from the first 92, because they focus directly on the Lordship of Jesus Christ who is our everything. For without Him, we did not come into existence, and can do nothing; but with Him, all things are possible. [John 1:3; John15:5; Matthew 19:26]

One may ask: "Why do we need man to testify to God's greatness or awesomeness?" After all, His Majesty can look after Himself, and His Name, His reputation and His Glory.

Indeed, man exists to point other men and women to God, through our lives and testimonies. This is the very purpose of these testimonies, to point to God and testify that He is the One, from Whom all of us come from, and to Whom all of us will return, and hence, is and should be our focus, all the days of our life.

Jesus is the Son of God. In Him and through Him, we are all now sons and daughters of the Living God, restored to our rightful original position as children of God, for we indeed came from God.

Jesus is the only begotten Son of God, and He and the Father are ONE.

References in the Bible that Jesus is the Son of God appears over fifty times in the New Testimony.

The most powerful and direct testimony is from our Father as the Spirit of God spoke during the Baptism of Jesus by John the Baptist.

Matthew 3:17, "And suddenly a voice from Heaven, saying, **'This is My beloved Son, in whom I am well pleased."**

This was repeated in the presence of Peter, recorded in Matthew 17:5, "This is My beloved Son in whom I am well pleased. Hear Him."

Three more verses in Mark 1:11, Luke 3:22, and 2 Peter 1:17 refer to and repeat the same exact words.

The first person privileged to know the true identity of Jesus as the Son of God, well before John the Baptist's testimony, without a doubt goes to the Blessed Mother of Jesus, Mother Mary, as recorded in Luke 1:35 below:

And the angel answered and said to her, "The Holy Spirit will come upon you, and the power of the Highest will overshadow you; therefore, also, that Holy One who is to be born will be called the **Son of God**."

For the disciples, it took several signs and miracles before they realized that Jesus was the Son of God. The first among them to realize this awesome truth was perhaps Peter when he saw Jesus stop the storm with a rebuke, recorded in Matthew 14:33, and reaffirmed again in Matthew 16:16, "You are the Christ, the Son of the Living God."

At the Cross of Calvary, when Jesus had laid down His Life, and the earthquake and thunder that happened soon after made them conclude in their spirits, "Truly this was the Son of God!" [Matthew 27:54.]

Mark's Gospel, the first sentence of the first Chapter declared, "The beginning of the gospel of Jesus Christ, the Son of God.

Later on, during the Ministry of Jesus, the unclean spirits cried out, "You are the Son of God." Mark 3:11

It is the Son of God who laid down His Life on Calvary to save the mankind from their sin and obtained and purchased eternal everlasting life for all of us.

John 3:16, "For God so loved the world that He gave His only begotten Son, that whoever believes in Him should not perish but have everlasting life."

Finally, as the proof of the pudding, the evidence recorded in history of mankind, Jesus the Son of God came and walked on earth, and when he prayed and touched them, the blind could see, the lame could walk and dead were resurrected.

He Himself laid down His life for three days, and was resurrected and seen by many witnesses, and on His final day on earth, He ascended or flew up into the clouds of Heaven as seen by many witnesses.

We do not doubt the existences of Plato, Socrates, Buddha, Confucius, Lao Tzu, all of whom existed and lived before Jesus of Nazareth, so too there is no doubt that all that Jesus did and was and testified to is recorded in the Scriptures.

He is the Son of God.

The Son rose up to Heaven so that our Father in Heaven could send down the Holy Spirit to us. And the powerful Third Person of the Holy Spirit, together with our Father God, THE LORD and His Son Jesus, now dwells in our physical body, as the Spirit of Christ in us.

Jesus did not leave us as orphans, as the Holy Spirit now lives in us. Jesus has also left us with His Powerful Name to be used in prayer, declaration and as His Name to call upon, and all we ask for will be granted to us.

The Name of Jesus is all powerful.

In His Name, we can move mountains, still the roaring oceans, stop the rain, and bring rainfall and more. There is awesome power in the Name of Jesus (Testimony # 076 and others)

In the days of the past, the king would carry out his laws through his officials. This was long before the days of multimedia and the press. His officer dressed in royal attire, on a royal horse would sound the trumpet in a square, lift up a scroll, and declare the King's statute or new law. His authority is legitimized by a seal, a signet ring to show that he represents the king.

In these days, since the coming of the Son, - the Son of God, God's authority is given to us through His Name – the Name of Jesus.

Jesus said in **Matthew 28:18, "All authority has been given to Me in heaven and on earth."**

Jesus has given the promise and confirmation that whatever we ask in His Name, it will be done. In John 14:13, **Jesus said: "And whatever you ask in My name, that I will do, that the Father may be glorified in the Son.**

Again, Jesus said in **John 14:14 "If you ask anything in My name, I will do it."**

Also, in John 15:16, and again in **John 16:23 "Whatever you ask the Father in My name, He may give you."**

Therefore, in these days, since the coming of our Savior and Lord Jesus, He has given His Name as His seal, signet ring, authority, scroll or scepter to ask our Father in Heaven, and it will be done.

His Name is all powerful, and truly able to do miracles, heal, open doors and shut doors, and for that reason, we should never use or say His Name, the Name of Jesus in vain. This is the second commandment, which is so important for all of us in Christ to understand and follow.

Truly, truly, His Name - the Name of Jesus is powerful. Use it with awe, reverence and with sincerity and love, from the depths of your heart.

Testimony # 094   Jesus my Friend

Jesus said in **John 15:15, "No longer do I call you servants, for a servant does not know what his master is doing; but I have called you friends, for all things that I heard from My Father I have made known to you."**

He continues by saying in the next two verses, "You did not choose Me, but I chose you and appointed you that you should go and bear fruit, and that your fruit should remain, that whatever you ask the Father in My name He may give you."

"These things I command you, that you love one another."

How has Jesus proven as truly "my best friend"?

Firstly, Jesus died on the Cross of Calvary, shedding His Blood, for the redemption of my sins, and thus He saved my life. [Testimony # 056 How I Found God]

He showed two situations in my dreams where He was present to personally save me.
[# 004   Jesus Helps me Escape and # 005   Jesus Saves me from a Beast]

Two Scripture verses confirmed that Jesus is always by our side, and with us till the end of time.

Psalm 16:8 "Because He is at my right hand, I shall not be moved."

Matthew 28:20 "I am with you always; even to the end of age."

Thus, I can rest assured that He is by my side, always as my Friend.

In fact, many have seen Jesus by my side. See "# 003 Jesus Standing beside me."

Truly, truly, Jesus has declared that we are friends, and He reveals to us whatever God, our Father tells Him, the Son. As we nurture this friendship, we are assured of His friendship, for Jesus is a true Friend who died for us, and who will never fail us nor forsake us. [Hebrews 13:5]

Testimony # 095   Jesus my Provider

Psalm 23 says, "The Lord is my shepherd; I shall not want."

That means that Jesus, my Lord and Shepherd looks after me and all my needs, and hence, I really do not need anything, as long as He is with me and I am by His side.

Again, in Matthew 6:25,26, Jesus Himself assures us, "Therefore I say to you, do not worry about your life, what you will eat or what you will drink; nor about your body, what you will put on. Is not life more than food and the body more than clothing?"

"Look at the birds of the air, for they neither sow nor reap nor gather into barns; yet your heavenly Father feeds them. Are you not of more value than they?"

Matthew 6:27-34 further adds, "Which of you by worrying can add one cubit to his stature? So why do you worry about clothing? Consider the lilies of the field, how they grow: they neither toil nor spin; and yet I say to you that even Solomon in all his glory was not arrayed like one of these.

"Now if God so clothes the grass of the field, which today is, and tomorrow is thrown into the oven, will He not much more clothe you? O you of little faith?

"Therefore, do not worry, saying, 'What shall we eat?' or 'What shall we drink?' or 'What shall we wear?'
"For after all these things the Gentiles seek. For your heavenly Father knows that you need all these things.

"But seek first the kingdom of God and His righteousness, and all these things shall be added to you.

"Therefore, do not worry about tomorrow, for tomorrow will worry about its own things. Sufficient for the day is its own trouble."

I felt it necessary to quote from verses 27 to 34, as the whole issue is explained very well here, by the Master Himself, and He is the Master of the whole Universe, for all things were made through Him, and without Him, was not anything made that was made. [John 1.3]

Truly, truly, God has made man, and made man master of the whole earth, and we are not alone. Our Lord and Savior Jesus is with us, all throughout, and one of His promises is that He will provide.

The air that we breathe, with the oxygen being 21% in every corner of the earth, and in every home day or night, the water from the skies and the seas, the earth that we live in and all that it produces, and more.

Man is precious in God's eyes, and we are certainly under His watchful eyes.

Luke 12:7 affirms, "But the very hairs of your head are all numbered. Do not fear therefore; you are of more value than many sparrows."

Our Father will not let us, his children die from hunger or thirst. Testimony # 017 'God's Hand is

Not Short' and others testify to His Majestic provision.

The key is to trust in Him, and put His kingdom and righteousness first, and the provisions and blessings will shower you and your family, in abundance.

Do not give the adversary the slightest opportunity to rob, steal or destroy what is yours.

The truth is: "God has promised to provide for all our needs. We can truly trust in Him, as His promises are sure and true." Psalm 118:8

Testimony # 096   Jesus my Healer

We are mortals, and everyone and anyone can fall sick.

On average, a child may be hit by a viral illness, about ten times a year, even with breast feeding and an effective vaccination program. An adult also can be afflicted with a viral illness, e.g. an influenza attack or common cold attack about twice a year.

Also, on average in every two years, a new virus arrives into the world, from mutation or through some biological transmission.

Sickness, poverty and all forms of depravity will continue in this world until our LORD returns in His Glory.

When the LORD sent the plaque, the locust, the frogs, the gnats to Egypt, He did not remove those creatures after that. Likewise, when thousands and thousands of snakes were biting the people in the desert, Moses complained and pleaded with the LORD. He did not remove the snakes, but provided a solution. He asked Moses to set up a bronze symbol of a snake, so that when the people were bitten by a snake, and they looked at the bronze statue of the snake (symbolic of the coming Healer), they were instantly healed.

So, sickness is here to stay. The LORD has provided a solution for He is the Healer.

The LORD is our Healer.

Exodus 23:25, "So you shall serve the LORD your God, and He will bless your bread and your water; And I will take sickness away from the midst of you."

When Jesus came down, live and ministered on earth, He healed the sick everywhere He went, and He healed everyone. Literally the whole village would come for His meetings, and everyone would leave healed, restored and well.

Exodus 15:26, "I am the LORD who heals you."

My testimonies are all listed above including # 021 God is my Healer, # 061, # 089 and many others.

The truth is that "God, the LORD is our Healer."

Testimony # 097   Jesus my Deliverer & Bailor

Jesus came to set the captives free. I make no excuse if this testimony is a teaching and preaching, for the Word of God is clear that my Lord Jesus is our deliverer and even bailor, when we fail and fall. He came to set us free.

Luke 4:18, "The Spirit of the LORD is upon Me, because He has anointed Me to preach the gospel to the poor; He has sent Me to heal the brokenhearted, to proclaim liberty to the captives. And recovery of sight to the blind, to set at liberty those who are oppressed; to proclaim the acceptable year of the LORD."

Jesus came and fulfilled the promise of Isaiah 61:1.

This is one of the most powerful truths and declarations of Jesus, as our Lord and Savior. Mankind as a whole had been kept as captives, trapped and unable to get out, till Jesus came to set the captives free.

The act of setting the 'captives' free is the key reason that Jesus, the Son of God came down on earth, and He paid the ransom, and won the victory on the Cross in Calvary, and said to our Father, "It is finished!"

Job done. Access to Heaven opened. Ransom paid in full. All are now bought over with a price - the life of the Son of God (1 Corinthians 6:20)

All prisoners set free – prisoners of sin, prisoners of death, prisoners of crime and blood shed, prisoners of conscience and guilt, prisoners of spiritual oppression, prisoners of addiction, gambling, deviation, pornography, craving for sex and various perversions, alcoholism, drugs and even greed, jealousy, love for money, all forms of captivity, including bondage, fear and depression – Jesus came to set the captives free.

The whole of mankind from the beginning of time to the end is now free, and all our sins washed away clean by the "Blood of the Lamb of God" – the Blood of Jesus.

Because of man's original sin, man was forever trapped and unable to make it into the Kingdom of Heaven, and unable to face our Heavenly Father.

God's Masterplan was drawn out to save mankind, and despite prophet after prophet, man continue to fall and fail. Finally, God had to send His Son, as the 'Sacrificial Lamb' to die on the Cross for the sins of mankind, thus paying off their sins with an eternal ransom, the Blood of His Only Son shed on Calvary.

That act of justification once and for all set the whole of mankind free, free from sin, free from captivity, free from the accusations of the adversary, and free from jail.

John 8:36 declares, "Therefore if the Son makes you free, you shall be free indeed."

Knowing the Word of God, knowing the truth, receiving it, claiming it and living it is the key for a successful Christian life.

John 8:32 "And you shall know the truth, and the truth shall make you free."

On earth, in one's lifetime, man may be oppressed, suppressed, trapped, bound or addicted, shattered, imprisoned, incarcerated, or even guilty, rise up and claim the powerful redemption by the Blood of the Lamb, in the Name of Jesus, and then and there, you are instantly set free.

Whether possessed, severely oppressed or even demonized spiritually, or whatever the situation, the powerful Name of Jesus alone can set the man or woman free, and free forever.

For freedom, Christ has set you free.

Psalm 146:7 "Who executes justice for the oppressed; Who gives food to the hungry? The LORD gives freedom to the prisoners."

As the Word says, the "law kills", for who can fulfill the law. Romans 8:2 says, "For the law of the Spirit of life in Christ Jesus has made me free from the law of sin and death."

Thus, Paul urges us to realize that we must not go back to sin and bondage, as Christ has already set us free. Galatians 5:1 "Stand fast therefore in the liberty by which Christ has made us free, and do not be entangled again with a yoke of bondage."

There are also many situations when one does wrong, and pays the penalty of it, and ends up in prison, and it is still the LORD who will bail you out. He forgives, and sets you free. Why go back to prison, and be entangled again with a yoke of bondage?

The truth is that "Jesus came to set the captives free. God is our deliverer and redeemer. When we know that, receive it, we are now free, and should stay free, away from sin and bondage.

Testimony # 098   Jesus my Protector

The LORD is our protector and shield. As all authority in Heaven and earth is with the Son, Jesus, the Lord Jesus is our protector.

I believe that everyone, and I really believe 'everyone' and every child has angels, who represent the LORD in protecting each one individually. This is related in testimony # 009 Encounter with Angels.

Psalm 91 is so true and relevant for everyone, in our walk on earth, knowingly or unknowingly. Why does everyone need angels? One is that the adversary is bent on stealing, killing, and destroying. It is his modus operandi all the time.

But the LORD's divine protection is secure and assured. Nevertheless, the risks are there. This author has had at least 7-8 near fatal situations, and indeed am very thankful for His divine protection.

Of course, we refer to physical protection, for the protection and preservation of our soul, our lives in eternity is assured, once we are in Christ.

John 3:16 "For God so loved the world, that He gave His only begotten Son, so that whoever believes in Him will not perish but will have everlasting life."

Matthew 10:28 "Do not fear those who kill the body but cannot kill the soul. But rather fear Him who is able to destroy both soul and body in hell."

Finally, we live for Christ to do His Work, as we are reminded by Paul in Philippians 1:21 "For to me, to live is Christ, and to die is gain."

Thus, our Lord Jesus is our Divine Protector, and we will not perish physically, as long as it is not yet time, and His angels will guard over us, each and every one of us.

We, of course, as individuals cannot be foolhardy, and take extraordinary risks, and too often, for we will be injured, if not killed when we do so.

Listen to the voice of God, as He will warn you.

See testimony # 012 Adrift in Pacific Ocean.

The truth is: "God is always by our side", and hence our protector. Psalm 16:8

Testimony # 099   Jesus my Savior

This is the greatest testimony, and the greatest miracle of all the testimonies related – the miracle of my salvation, or the miracle of being saved, and that is that we are now transferred from the death list to the Eternal Life list.

My name, our names are etched and securely written in the Book of Life; this Book is the list of all those who can make it to Heaven, those who are eligible to enter Heaven.

It is almost true to the fact and point that at the Entry point or Immigration Center in Heaven, there will be a final check to see if your name and mine are written in this Book of Life.

This is not a joke, or a laughing matter, as every second, one or two persons on earth die and face the reality of meeting God, our Maker. He has His criteria for entry into the Gates of Heaven. The criteria are very strict, and the standards are very high – total purity, totally free from sin, and completely washed of any evil or crime.

In other words, the wages of sin are death, and none are eligible, except by the Grace of God, by the Mercy of God, by His Royal Pardon, which thankfully and compassionately has been wrought and bought by none other than the Son of God Himself.

Jesus, the Son of God is our Passport, our Visa, our PASSWORD, the Passover Lamb and the Word of God. That is exactly what the Gospel is saying, and no other faith or religion offers that kind of statement, declaration and free entry by just declaring one Name, the only Name by which everyone and anyone can be saved.

The Bible says clearly, that there is no other name by which one is saved, except by the name of Jesus.

Acts 4:12 "Nor is there salvation in any other, for there is no other name under heaven given among men by which we must be saved."

John 20:31 "but these are written that you may believe that Jesus is the Christ, the Son of God, and that believing you may have life in His Name."

John 1:12 "But as many as received Him, to them He gave the right to become children of God, to those who believe in His Name; who were born, not of blood, nor of the will of the flesh, nor of the will of man, but of God."

How much more explicit or implicit can the Gospel be, when it says that Jesus and God are one, and that Jesus is the Son of God, who came down to pay our ransom, and that only in His Name, can we be saved.

And, it is free, all paid for. You do not need to go any penance, pay any sacrifice, only repent of your sins, and believe and receive Jesus as your Savior.

Salvation through Jesus is already achieved by the Grace of God. Salvation is a miracle in itself; and to be able to believe is a miracle truly.

Many people pay a hefty price to believe, as they are persecuted till death.

Many communities are condemned or obstructed from believing from birth until physical death; yet many boldly rise up to declare that they are now Christians and dare to call God, their Father in Heaven.

It is however all through the working of the Spirit of God, the Holy Spirit who convinces and convicts the unbeliever to become a believer and follower of Jesus Christ.

Yet, you and I need to hear the message, the Good News, for without hearing, how can one know? The truth has to be told and taught, and message when reaching the heart, will churn and convict, and with the working of the Holy Spirit, a new soul is ushered into the Kingdom of God, saved by Grace, and is now "Born Again" into the Kingdom of God, all through just one act : "Belief in Jesus."

Jesus, the Son of God is my Lord and Savior and the Savior of the World. There is no other person who can do this work, who needs to do this work, for all authority in heaven and on earth is now in the Hands of Jesus.

Matthew 28:18 "And Jesus came and spoke to them, saying, "All authority has been given to Me in heaven and on earth.""

This is what Jesus said, and He is the Son of God, not a mad man, not a cheat or a liar.

He laid down His life to be crucified to pay for the sins of mankind, and He took back His Life and rose again on the third day. All these were witnessed and recorded and is true. The tomb was empty.

Just as the teachings and historical facts about Plato, Socrates, Buddha, Confucius and Lao Tzu are true, and they all came well before Jesus, - so too are the Gospels, and we living ones continue to testify to that truth.

I have followed Jesus faithfully for over 38 years now, and I know in my heart that He is my Lord and Savior and I will meet Him one day, Face to face in Heaven, where He is enthroned on High with our Father in Heaven.

I and all those who believe in Jesus, know in our hearts and we can hold our right hand on our chest and declare that "I know that on the final day, I will enter Heaven because my Savior is there to greet and welcome me HOME. His name is Jesus, the Son of God, the Co-Creator of the Heavens and the earth, the Chief Judge and Savior of the World, the King of Heaven.

The truth is: "Jesus is the Way, the Truth and the Life, and no one comes to the Father but through Me (Jesus)" John 14:6, which means that "Jesus is Savior for mankind, hence the Way to Heaven, also the Truth, and the true abundant life is in Him.

Testimony # 100   Jesus my Beloved

Finally, all that really matters is my beloved, the lover of my soul, and His Name is Jesus. My beloved is mine and I am His.

All these testimonies are true and are being told for one reason and one purpose, to tell all the readers that the most important person in my life is "Jesus", for He loves me with all His heart, mind and soul, as He laid down His life for me.

He loved me first, and in reciprocation, I love Him, my beloved Jesus with all my heart, all my mind and all my soul.

The one who loved me most, loves not just me, the person and personality, not my physical self or body, which only lasts a few decades, but is the lover of my soul, which is for eternity.

Everything on earth, including me and you come from Him, from Jesus, who was from the beginning the Co-Creator of the earth and the heavens and all that is in it.

Without Him, without Jesus, nothing came into being, for all things were made through Jesus.

John 1:2,3 "He was in the beginning with God. All things were made through Him, and without Him, nothing was made that was made."

Apart from Jesus, I am nothing, and can do nothing.

But, with Him and in Him, I can do all things.

Loving Jesus means, to understand who He is, know who He is, and to put Jesus first above all things, and surrender totally to Him; and whatever we say, do, think and act or feel, we relate and are responsible to Him.

Our DNA is from Jesus, our life, our breath, our very being is from Him. It is natural and obvious then to love Him, as He loves me and you, for we are His own, or we belong to Him, as we belong to Him, and He belongs to us.

The truth is: "Jesus is my beloved, and my beloved is mine." Songs of Solomon 6:3

Jesus is my first love, my lover – the Lover of my soul, for He first love us from the beginning of time.

This is the Testimony of Jesus, the Son of God.

When you call upon Jesus, and pray in His Name to our Father in Heaven, all your prayers will be answered.

May **"The End"** of this book be the start of a new beginning for you.

The Author

Dr Timothy Sng was born in Kluang, Johor in Malaysia in 1951. Thirty years later, he was born again in the Lord Jesus Christ on 18th of October, 1981. Baptized by full emersion took place in SIB Iris Garden, Kuching a year later, followed by the baptism of the Holy Spirit in 1982.

As a fulltime neurologist initially in public later in private practice, he moved to the capital city of Kuala Lumpur in 1991, and has remained there since.

Apart from winning souls for Jesus, now in excess of 500 on a personal one-to-one basis, Dr Sng's has a keen passion in 'writing', a talent he discovered some three decades ago. Over the years, the doors opened for teaching and sharing, from lunch meetings to Sunday service, to evangelistic meetings and church camps.

The combination of teaching and a passion for writing, with revelation from The Spirit of God, has enabled some 15 eBooks to be published in Amazon, Smashwords and other portals.

It is the publication of 'The Good Son' in April 2019 as the first book by Timothy Sng, that marks the birth of a Christian author and writer.

This latest title "The Testimony of Jesus" – Releasing the spirit of prophecy through, `Amazing Christian Testimonies & Studies' hopes to reach the far corners of the earth, as it is indeed a 'work commissioned by God' when Jesus said, "Go!"

And it will! May this latest work be a catalyst to spark of the readers to do greater works for the LORD.

Look out for the coming titles:

Trilogy (February 2020)
In Search of the Living God & Beyond
Jesus, The Son of God
The Return of The Messiah

Pleasing our Father in Heaven (`The Good Son' to be republished in March 2020)
When Crisis or Disaster Strikes (April 2020)
Your Faith makes The Difference (May 2020)

Second Trilogy (August 2020)
The Ambassador of Christ in You
Being a Successful Fisher of Men
The Marketplace Minister

Imitate me - The key to Discipleship (October 2020)

Understanding the Mind, Body & Spirit (December 2020)
Father, Son & Holy Spirit (February 2021)
Man is Mind (April 2021)
Thy Word is a Lamp to my feet (Verses I memorize and use) June 2021

Matthew 19:26 "With men this is impossible, but with God all things are possible."